DEFG

MNO

UVWXY

Z-Z-Z-Z-Z-Z-Z-Z-Z-Z

GW00597270

Fairy Tale Picture Dictionary

Fairy Tale Picture Dictionary

Jane Wilton-Smith
illustrated by Kilmeny Niland

HODDER AND STOUGHTON
SYDNEY LONDON AUCKLAND TORONTO

INTRODUCTION

Sooner or later a child will want to put into words a feeling or thought which is important to him. To do this he will need the "right" words — words which say what *he* wants to say. But English is a powerful and difficult language, rich with words of many shades of meaning. It is spiced with confusing words such as "back" — "back a horse", "pay back", "lean back", "go back", "backbone", etc. It is peppered with conjunctions and prepositions which often baffle even an articulate adult. Hard-working words such as "some" or "any" can be demonstrated in a sentence and young children will also use them accurately in speech. But can we be sure that they are making a meaningful contribution to the child's language and reading fluency?

Over-simplication can also be confusing. So Jane Wilton-Smith, a former teacher, provides the stimulus of a traditional story, first to involve the child, then to extend the understanding of variations in word meanings. Selected words are explained both in the context of the story and in everyday use. Story and definitions are enriched by Kilmeny Niland's sensitive and enchanting illustrations. Often an illustration can define more accurately than a paragraph of words so illustrations and words are interwoven, one re-inforcing the other. It is a beguiling combination.

This guileful simplicity is hard to achieve. Jane Wilton-Smith and Kilmeny Niland have not over-stepped a small child's interests; yet they contrive to communicate something of the pleasure and fun of words. The picture dictionary format is readily accepted in our visually oriented age of mass media for both adults and children. This one was compiled with a lively awareness of the value of enjoyment — learning painlessly. The result will not be dismissed as "boring". It is a dictionary to enjoy.

Jean Chapman

First published in 1979 by Hodder and Stoughton (Australia) Pty Limited,
2 Apollo Place, Lane Cove, NSW 2066
in association with Hodder and Stoughton Children's Books,
Mill Road, Dunton Green, Sevenoaks, Kent, England

© text, Hodder and Stoughton (Australia) Pty Limited, 1979
© illustrations, Kilmeny Niland, 1979

This book is copyright. Apart from any fair dealing for the purposes of private study, research, criticism or review as permitted under the Copyright Act, no part may be reproduced by any process without written permission. Inquiries should be addressed to the publishers.

National Library of Australia Cataloguing-in-Publication entry

Wilton-Smith, Jane
    Fairy Tale Picture Dictionary
    For children ISBN 0 340 23240 4
    1. English language — Dictionaries, Juvenile 1. Niland, Kilmeny, Illus. 11. Title
423.024'054
Typeset by G.T. Setters, Lane Cove
Printed in Singapore

Aladdin and his Wonderful Lamp

Aladdin lived many years ago in China, with his widowed mother. They were very poor.

One day a tall dark Magician came and told Aladdin that he was his long-lost uncle. If Aladdin wanted to be rich he must follow him.

Soon they arrived at a wooden trapdoor in the ground. The Magician gave Aladdin a magic ring to wear on his finger. He said it would keep him safe when he went into the cave beneath the trapdoor. He was to search for a lamp there, and bring it back.

Aladdin did as he was told. He found the lamp and many beautiful jewels hanging on trees and carried them back to the Magician.

The Magician commanded Aladdin to pass him up the ring and the lamp. He looked so fierce that Aladdin was afraid his uncle would not help him out of the cave. They argued loudly, and then the Magician shut the trapdoor and left Aladdin by himself.

It was very dark in the cave and Aladdin was frightened. He brushed a tear from his cheek, and as he did so he touched it with the magic ring. A great Genie appeared who said he could grant wishes. Of course, Aladdin wished to go home.

Next day Aladdin's mother was rubbing the old lamp to make it shine. Another great Genie appeared and said HE could grant wishes too.

Aladdin wished for a big house to live in. The Genie of the Lamp made him a Prince and gave him a grand castle.

A few years later Aladdin fell in love with a rich Sultan's daughter, and married her. The Magician was jealous. He tricked Aladdin's new wife into giving him the magic lamp and then whisked the castle and everyone in it from China to Africa!

But Aladdin still had his magic ring. With the help of the Genie of the Ring the Magician was killed and all Aladdin's possessions were restored to him.

able

The Genie of the Lamp was **able** to grant wishes. He could do whatever Aladdin wanted.

about

Aladdin was trapped in the cave for **about** four hours. He did not know **about** the Genie of the Lamp.

ache

Aladdin had an **ache**, a pain, in his hand from banging at the trapdoor. His hand hurt.

across

How do you get **across** the road? You make sure there are no cars coming and go from one side to the other. You walk quickly and carefully.

aeroplane

An **aeroplane** is a large flying machine that carries people and goods from one place to another.

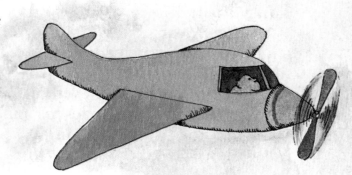

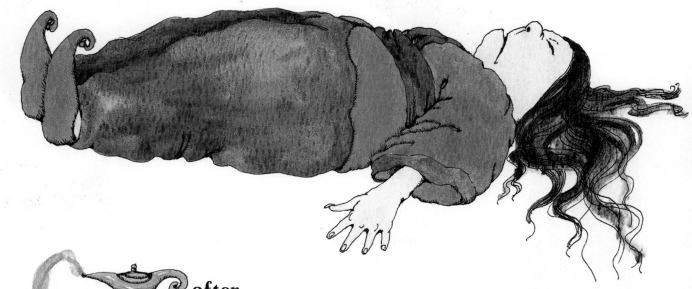

after
Aladdin's mother fainted with fright **after** the Genie of the Lamp appeared.

afternoon
Afternoon comes after 12 o'clock midday and before evening.

again
Aladdin was very pleased to see his mother **again**, once more, after his adventure in the cave.

ago
The story of Aladdin was first told a long time **ago.**

air
Air is all around us. We can't see it but we have to breathe it to live. Feel **air** by blowing on your finger.

alive
You are **alive**. Animals and plants and people are **alive** because they live and breathe. They are not dead.

all
All means every single one. **All** the trees in the cave were covered with precious jewels.

alligator
Aladdin would not have seen an **alligator** in his country. **Alligators** are reptiles that live in rivers in America.

allow
"O, Sultan, the great Prince Aladdin begs that you will **allow** him to visit your palace," said Aladdin's mother. "He wants you to let him come."

alone
Aladdin thought he had been left **alone** and was now by himself in the cave. Was that true?

already
Aladdin's Magician Uncle was rich before he went to the cave. He **already** had lots of treasure. How do you think he got it?

always

Always is all the time. A kangaroo **always** has a long tail. Night **always** comes after day.

another

Jack and the Beanstalk is **another** story, one more story, about a boy with a magic gift.

answer

When you ask a question you expect an **answer**. Is there a rabbit on this page? The **answer** is 'No'.

any

If you could choose **any** story you wanted to hear would you need **any** help? **Any** means one or some.

anything

Is there **anything** Aladdin can do to the wicked Magician to get his castle back? Yes, there is something. What is it?

anyway

Aladdin still had his magic ring, **anyway**. Whatever happened he could use it to trick the wicked Magician.

apple

An **apple** is a delicious fruit with a red or green skin.

April

April is the fourth month of the year. It comes after March.

arm
Your **arm** is part of your body. It is between your shoulder and your hand. You have two **arms**. What can you do with them?

around
When Aladdin had climbed into the cave he looked **around** him. There were glittering jewels on the trees and flowers on all sides of him.

as
As soon **as** the magician saw Aladdin come back with the jewels he wanted to take the magic ring and the lamp from him.

ask
You **ask** a question when you want to know something.

asleep
Aladdin was so tired after his adventure in the cave that he fell **asleep** very quickly that night. Do you dream when you are **asleep**?

August
August is the eighth month of the year. It comes after July.

awake
Aladdin was wide **awake** early in the morning. He had woken up from his sleep.

away
The wicked Magician whisked Aladdin's castle **away** from China to the middle of Africa. Aladdin was very annoyed that it had gone.

10

Bb   Beauty and the Beast

There was once a man who had three daughters. One day he had to ride to the far-off town and he asked his daughters what they would like him to bring them. The two eldest wanted jewellery, but the youngest, whose name was Beauty, wanted only a rose.

The man finished his business in the town and set off for home. He thought he would leave the rose until he was nearly there, so that it would be fresh.

But after a while he was caught in a terrible storm and lost his way. He found himself outside a big house and heard a voice say, "Come inside."

In he went, and saw a table laid with all sorts of good things to eat. The voice told him to help himself, so he did.

The storm passed and he set off again, stopping to pick a rose from the garden. All at once a hideous beast sprang on him, very angry that the man had taken a flower. He would not let him go until the man promised to give him the very first thing he set his eyes on when he got home.

Of course, Beauty was the first thing he set his eyes on! So she had to go and live with the Beast.

Although the Beast was ugly, he was kind and he gave Beauty a magic mirror in which she could see her father and sisters. Several weeks later Beauty saw that her father was ill and begged the Beast to let her go home. He agreed, as long as she returned as soon as she could.

Beauty was so happy to be home that she forgot her promise to the Beast, until she looked in the mirror again and saw him lying on the floor, crying. She ran all the way to his house and when she saw him she was so sad that she threw her arms around him and kissed him.

All at once the Beast sprang up from the ground, transformed into a handsome prince. Beauty's kiss had broken a wicked spell cast upon the Prince by a witch.

So Beauty and the Prince were married and lived happily together for the rest of their lives.

baby

A **baby** is a very young child.

back

Beauty asked her father to bring a rose **back** with him when he returned. He jumped up on to his horse's **back** and rode away.

backwards

When Beauty looked into the mirror she saw that the Beast was so weak he had fallen down **backwards**. He had fallen on his back.

bad

Bad is not good. A robber steals things that are not his. He is a **bad** man.

badge

A **badge** is a sign. It can tell what a person does or what the place is. A policeman wears a **badge**. So do boy scouts and bus conductors and football teams.

bag

Beauty packs her things into a large **bag** and goes to live with the Beast.

ball

A **ball** is round and is used for games. You can hit it, or throw it, or bounce it.

balloon

A **balloon** is made of thin rubber. Fill it with air by blowing into it. Have fun with it! If you prick it, it will burst.

banana

A **banana** is long and yellow. Is it your favourite fruit?

band

When Beauty and the prince were married a **band** of musicians played at the wedding. Beauty wore a **band** of pink roses around her hair and a gold wedding **band** on her finger.

basket

Beauty carried a **basket** of roses too.

bat

A **bat** is used to play cricket and other games. A **bat** is also a flying animal that likes fruit (especially bananas) and eats it mostly at night.

bath

You need a **bath** to wash off the dirt when you have been playing outside all day. A **bath** makes you clean.

battery

A **battery** makes electricity. A car has a **battery**, so has a torch and a transistor radio.

beach

The **beach** is a good place to go in hot weather. You can go in the water to keep cool and you can play on the sand.

beads

Beauty's elder sister wanted a string of **beads** from her father to wear around her neck.

beak

A **beak** is a bird's bill. It is strong and sharp to catch food with, carry things in and for fighting.

13

bean
A **bean** is a long green vegetable.

bear
A **bear** is a black or brown furry animal.
Some **bears** are very fierce. Does the Beast look a little like a **bear**?

beat
The cook **beat** up the cake for Beauty's wedding. Do you remember the band of musicians? The drummer **beat** his drum loudly.

beautiful
Beauty got her name because she had a **beautiful** face and a sweet temper.

because
Why did the Beast change into a handsome prince? He changed **because** Beauty kissed him.

bed

A **bed** is good to lie down on when you are tired.

bee

A **bee** is a black and yellow striped insect with wings. It gathers honey and nectar from flowers and lives in a hive.

before

The Beast was very ugly **before** he was changed into a handsome prince.

beg

To **beg** is to plead for something. Beauty **begged** the Beast to let her see her father again.

behind

Beauty's father picked a rose from the Beast's garden. He was frightened by a roar from **behind** him.

bell

The church **bell** rang to summon the people to the wedding.

bend
Can you **bend** over and touch your toes? **Bent** is not straight.

best
A rose, a pansy or a daffodil. Which flower do you like **best**? Which is your favourite?

better
When you are ill you must stay in bed until you are **better**. A broom is **better** than a spade for sweeping the floor.

big
A kangaroo is a **big** animal. A horse is **bigger**. An elephant is the **biggest** of all three.

bin
A **bin** can be used for keeping garbage, or bread, or flour in. **Bins** come in different sizes.

bird
A **bird** is an animal that has wings and can fly. What kind of a **bird** is this?

birthday

Your **birthday** is the day you were born. Each year on that day you are a year older.

biscuit

A **biscuit** is made from butter, eggs and flour. It is baked in the oven until it is crispy and crunchy.

bite

You **bite** with your teeth. Beauty's father is **biting** his piece of chicken.

black

Black is the colour of the cat's fur.

blanket

A **blanket** will keep you warm in bed on cold nights.

blow

You can **blow** by puffing air out of your mouth. Beauty's father was caught in a storm. The wind **blew** very strongly.

blue

Blue is the colour of the sea.

boat

A **boat** carries people and things on water. Boats can have sails, or oars, or engines.

body

Your **body** is all of you that can be seen
— head, legs, arms, feet, back, front.
Can you add any more?

bomb

A **bomb** is full of gunpowder. It explodes.

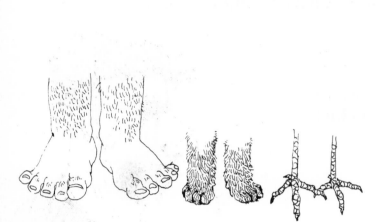

bone

The hard parts inside your body are
bones. Feel your toes. They have lots of
bones.

book

You are reading a **book** now. **Books** can tell you all sorts of different things.

boot

A **boot** is a very heavy shoe. Beauty's
father wore strong **boots** when he rode away from home.

born

The day you were **born** was your first day in the world — your birthday.

both

Beauty had two sisters. They were **both** older than she was.
Both means two.

bottle

A **bottle** is made of glass or plastic and
is for keeping drink or sauce in.
Anything liquid that runs out quickly
can be put in a **bottle**.

bottom

Beauty's father rode up to the top of
the hill. Then he rode down to the
bottom on his way home. The **bottom**
is the lowest part of something.

bounce

A rubber ball will **bounce**. The Beast
bounced up from the ground when
Beauty kissed him. That means he
moved as quickly as a rubber ball.

bowl

Here is a **bowl** of roses from the Beast's garden. Which colour do you like best?

bowling

Bowling is throwing a ball in a game like cricket.
You throw it in a special way for the batsman to hit.

box

Here is a **box** with a pearl necklace in it
for Beauty's elder sister.

boy

A **boy** is a man child. When he grows
up he will be a man.

branch

The **branch** of this rose bush is covered in roses.

brave

Beauty was very **brave** to stay with the
Beast because he frightened her.

bread

Bread is made of flour and yeast and is good to eat.

break

The Beast knew that if Beauty kissed
him she would **break** the spell. He
would turn into a prince again and the spell would be **broken**.

20

breakfast
What do you eat for **breakfast**? It is the first meal of the day.

brick
The Beast's house was built of many **bricks**. Is your house built of **bricks**? **Bricks** are made from clay, then baked very hard.

bridge
There is a **bridge** over the stream outside the Beast's house.

bright
Some of the roses in the garden are **bright** red. They look pretty in the **bright** sunshine.

bring
"Please **bring** me a rose, Father," said Beauty. "It will be light to carry here."

brother
Is there a boy in your family? If there is then he is your **brother**. Beauty had no **brothers**, only sisters.

brown
Brown is the colour of the gate.

brush

You clean your teeth with a **brush**. You **brush** your hair to keep it clean. Think of some other **brushes**.

bubble

Can you blow soap **bubbles**? They are balls of liquid full of air. Some are big, some are small.

bucket

A **bucket** is used for carrying water or sand. Have you got a **bucket** at home?

build

It must have taken a long time to **build** this castle with bricks. It is a very big **building**.

bump

Whoops! If you don't watch where you're going you might **bump** into something hard!

burn

Wood will **burn** on a barbecue fire. You must watch carefully or the steak might get too hot and be **burnt**.

bury

To **bury** something is to put it in the ground. Then it is covered with dirt or stones so that it cannot be seen.

butter

Butter is made from cream. It is yellow and we spread it on bread.

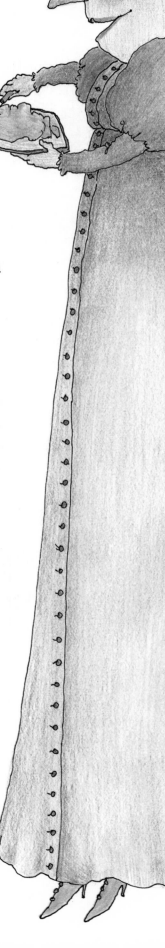

button

Shirts and coats can be done up with **buttons**. **Buttons** go through **buttonholes**. Have you **buttons** on your clothes?

buy

Beauty's father promised to **buy** presents for his daughters. He paid for the necklace and bracelet. He **bought** them.

24

Cc

Cinderella

There was once a man who had a beautiful and sweet-tempered daughter named Cinderella. When his first wife died he married another who was bad-tempered and whose two daughters were ugly and spiteful. The three of them made Cinderella do all the dirty jobs in the house.

One day the ugly sisters were delighted to receive an invitation to a Ball given by the King. They made Cinderella curl their hair and iron their dresses, thinking that they looked very beautiful for the Ball. In fact, Cinderella in her rags was more beautiful than they.

When they had gone Cinderella sat in the kitchen crying. Suddenly an old woman appeared and asked her if she was crying because she couldn't go to the Ball. Cinderella confessed that she was.

"I am your Fairy Godmother, Cinderella, and can make you ready for the Ball in no time," said the old lady; and with a wave of her wand she turned a pumpkin into a golden coach, two mice into prancing horses, a rat into a coachman, six lizards into footmen, and Cinderella's rags into the most beautiful ball gown you have ever seen, complete with a lovely pair of glass slippers!

Cinderella went off to the Ball, promising to return by midnight, when the spell would be broken. The Prince fell in love with her as soon as he saw her, and danced with her all evening. All the other ladies, including the ugly sisters, were *insanely* jealous.

When midnight struck Cinderella remembered the Fairy Godmother's words and ran home as quickly as she could. In her hurry she lost one of her glass slippers. This was the only clue the Prince had as to who she was, and he ordered that every girl in the kingdom must try it on. Whoever it fitted would be his wife.

The ugly sisters didn't want Cinderella to try on the slipper. They knew it would fit her. But the Royal Herald insisted that she try it on. Of course it fitted, and she married Prince Charming and lived happily ever after.

cabbage

A **cabbage** is a green leafy vegetable. It tastes good and is good for you too.

cake

A **cake** is delicious too, but not as good for you as cabbage.

calf

A **calf** is a baby cow or bull.

call

What is your name? What do people **call** you? Cinderella was **called** Cinderella because she used to sit huddled among the cinders in the chimney to keep warm.

camel

A **camel** is a large brown animal with a hump. It can live in the desert without water for quite a long time.

camera

You take photographs with a **camera**.
There are movie **cameras** that take films and still **cameras** that take prints or slides. Have you got a good photograph of yourself?

cap

Cinderella's wicked stepmother wore a
mob-**cap** in the house. There are all
sorts of **caps** that people can wear on
their heads. Policemen wear **caps**, so do nurses. Do you?

capsicum

A **capsicum** is a green or red vegetable with lots of seeds inside it.

captain

A **captain** is a leader of men in the army. A
captain commands a ship or a cricket team.
What else?

car

A motor **car** can carry you where you
want to go. It has four wheels and an
engine.

card

The ugly sisters received an invitation
card to the Ball. **Card** is stiff paper.

cardboard

Cardboard is even stiffer and thicker
than card.

care

"Take **care**!" cried the Fairy
Godmother. "Make sure you are back
by twelve o'clock!" To **take care** is to
pay attention to. To **take care of** means
to look after something or someone.

careful

Was Cinderella **careful** about watching
the time? Did she remember to look at
the clock and leave before twelve?

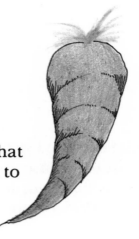

carrot

A **carrot** is a long orange vegetable that grows underground. Cinderella had to scrape the **carrots** for dinner.

carry

"You must **carry** this slipper to every girl in the kingdom," said the Prince to the Herald. "Take it in your hand and see whose foot it fits."

case

A **case** is made of wood or glass or leather. It is for carrying or storing things in. **Suitcases** hold clothes when you go on holiday.

cat

Tabby, ginger, black. **Cats** can be all these colours. Have you got a **cat**?

catch

"Go outside and **catch** six lizards behind the watering-can, Cinderella," said the Fairy Godmother. "Grab hold of them with your hands and when you have **caught** them bring them to me."

cauliflower

A **cauliflower** is a vegetable with a white head and green leaves. It is very good to eat. Do you like it?

cave

A **cave** is a hole in the rocks or underground. **Caves** are exciting to explore, but not on your own. Sometimes they **cave** in. That means the roof falls down and the hole fills up.

cement

Cement is used to stick bricks and stones together to make walls. It is used for floors too. Don't stand on wet **cement** or you'll stick to it!

cent

A **cent** is a coin. There are one hundred **cents** in a dollar.

chair

"Sit down on this **chair**, Cinderella," said the Royal Herald, "and try on this slipper."

chalk

Teachers use **chalk** to write on the blackboard. **Chalk** comes in lots of pretty colours.

chance

"Cinderella, would you like a **chance** to go to the Ball?" said the Fairy Godmother. "Oh yes, I would love to be able to go," replied Cinderella.

change

"But you can't go to the Ball in those rags, Cinderella. I will have to **change** your rags into something better." To **change** is to make different.

chase

"**Chase** after that beautiful girl!" called Prince Charming. "You must run after her and catch her."

check

"We must test this glass slipper on the foot of every girl in the kingdom," said Prince Charming. "We must **check** every girl to see if it fits."
Check can also mean to stop. It can be a pattern.

chest

Prince Charming looked very handsome at the Ball. He wore a frill across his **chest**.

chicken
A **chicken** is a baby hen or rooster.

child
A **child** is a young person. You are a **child**. You and your friends are **children**.

chimney
Cinderella had to sit in the **chimney** corner to keep warm. **Chimneys** take smoke out of a room into the air outside.

chip
If you **chip** something you break a small piece off.

chocolate
Chocolate is brown and sweet and delicious. But too much **chocolate** means stomach-aches and rotting teeth.

31

Christmas
Christmas day is December 25th. It is Jesus Christ's birthday.

circle
Cinderella and Prince Charming danced round and round in a **circle** in the great big ballroom. How many **circles** can you see around you?

class
When you go to school you are in a **class** with other children. A teacher teaches you in the **classroom**.

claw
A **claw** is an animal's fingernail. It is much stronger and sharper than our fingernails. Which animals have **claws**?

clean

Every day Cinderella had to stay at home and **clean** the house. She had to make sure there was no dirt anywhere.

clever

What a **clever** Fairy Godmother! Fancy being able to make Cinderella ready to go to the Ball so quickly! She must have worked very hard at her magic lessons when she was a young fairy.

climb

To **climb** is to go up. Cinderella **climbed** a lot of stairs on her way out of the Palace.

clock

Ding, dong! Twelve **o'clock**! The **clock** chimed twelve times to tell everyone that it was midnight. **Clocks** measure hours and minutes.

close

Prince Charming stayed **close** to
Cinderella all evening at the Ball. He
liked to be near her. When Cinderella
reached her attic room again she **closed**
the door and fell asleep on her bed. To
close is to shut.

clothes

The ugly sisters always wore pretty
clothes that fitted them well. They
made Cinderella wear rags. **Clothes**
protect our bodies. What **clothes** are
you wearing?

cloud

A **cloud** is made of moisture. It floats
across the sky until it is ready to send
rain down on the earth.

coat

The footmen on the golden coach wore smart **coats**.
Would you wear a **coat** on your legs? No? Then where?

cocoa

Cocoa is a brown powder made from
cocoa beans. It makes a delicious milky
drink and chocolate.

coconut

A **coconut** is the large seed from a palm
tree. If you can break it open you can
eat the delicious white flesh inside.

coffee
Coffee is a drink made from **coffee** beans.

cold
Poor Cinderella had to go home at midnight and sleep in her **cold** attic. It was not warm.

colour
The ballroom was a blaze of **colour**. Pink, blue, yellow, green. All the ladies in their **colourful** dresses were a beautiful sight.

come
"You must make sure you **come** home before midnight, Cinderella," said the Fairy Godmother. But Cinderella **came** running out of the ballroom at the very last minute and the spell was broken.

cook
Cinderella had to **cook** the meals every day for her two ugly sisters. Whatever she prepared they ate without even a thank-you.

copy

Find a piece of paper and a pencil.
Copy the picture of the brown horse.
Make it look just the same.

cord

A **cord** is a piece of string or rope.

cordial

Which is your favourite **cordial** to
drink in hot weather — lemon, lime or
orange?

corn

Corn is a yellow vegetable. **Corn-on-
the-cob** tastes delicious with butter.
You may need a bib to eat it tidily!

corner

A **corner** is where things such as two roads or two walls meet. Prince Charming ran out of the palace after Cinderella but she had already gone round the **corner**.

count

One ... two ... three ... four. What number can you **count** to?

couple

A **couple** means two. There were a **couple** of horses drawing Cinderella's coach. There were two.

cow

A **cow** is a farm animal that says
"Moo" and gives us milk.

crack

"**Crack**!" sounds the whip as the
coachman drives the horses to the
Palace. A **crack** is a fine break in a cup
or bowl. Or it is a very thin space
between two floorboards.

crash

"**Crash**!" That's what happens when
people hurry and don't look where
they are going. They bump into things.

crazy

"You are **crazy** if you think you can get
this glass slipper on," said the royal
herald to the ugly sisters. "You are
mad because it is impossible."

cream
Cream is the oily part of milk which comes to the top. Butter is made from **cream**.

creek
A **creek** is a stream of water. Some people fish in the **creek**.

cross
The two ugly sisters were very **cross** because they did not dance with Prince Charming all night. They were angry. **Crosses** can be signs or shapes of things, like these.

cry
"Don't **cry**, Cinderella," said the Fairy Godmother. "There is no need for tears. I can send you to the Ball."

cucumber
A **cucumber** is a long green-skinned salad vegetable.

cup
A **cup** is for drinking from. **Cups** stand on saucers.

cupboard
A **cupboard** is for keeping plates or toys or towels in. What do you keep in your **cupboard**?

cut
Knives and scissors are used to **cut** through food and paper and other things. Be careful with them or you might make a **cut** in your skin instead.

Dd

Dick Whittington
and his Cat

Dick Whittington lived in a country village. He thought that if he went to London he would find gold in the streets and become rich.

When he arrived in London he found that the rain was as wet, and the nights as cold, as in his village, and there was no gold in the streets. He would have gone home but he heard the church bells chiming:

> "Turn again, Whittington,
> Thou worthy citizen,
> Turn again, Whittington,
> Lord Mayor of London!"

Luckily for him he slept on the doorstep of a house where there lived a kind cook who took him in as a kitchen boy.

Dick bought himself a cat for company, and to catch rats, and dreamed about being Lord Mayor of London. His master was a merchant named Fitzwarren.

It was the custom in those days to send something for luck in a new ship. Fitzwarren's new ship was going to Africa to trade with a great Sultan. Fitzwarren told Dick to send something in it. Dick had only his cat. He sent that.

The African Sultan was amazed when the cat killed fifty rats in his palace, and offered the ship's captain a great sack of gold in exchange for it.

So Dick became very rich. He married Alice, Fitzwarren's daughter, and several years later he become Lord Mayor of London.

And all thanks to some bells and a cat.

dare
Will Dick Whittington **dare** to go back to London to seek his fortune? Will he be brave enough to do it?

dark
At night, when the sun goes down, it is **dark**. It is not light.

day
During the **day** it is light outside. When it gets dark it is night-time.

dear
A person we love is very **dear** to us. The Sultan paid a thousand gold pieces for Dick's cat. The cat was very **dear**.

December
December is the last month of the year. Christmas comes in **December**.

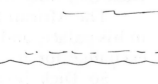

deep
The merchant's ship sailed across the sea. The sea was so **deep** that it was a very long way to the bottom.

desk
A **desk** is a special table for writing on.

die

A lot of flowers are **dead** in the winter. Their leaves and blooms go brown and **die**. They are not alive.

different

Dick Whittington decided to leave his village and live in a **different** place. He did not want to stay in the same place anymore.

dig

A gardener has to **dig** the earth with a spade or fork. He turns up the soil.

dinner

When Dick was a good boy Cook would give him a big slice of jam tart after his **dinner**. What is your favourite **dinner**?

dip

Some people like to go in the sea for a **dip**. Do you like being in the sea? To **dip** is to put something in a liquid and then take it out again. Or you can **dip** your hand into a purse.

dirt

Cook does not like **dirty** boys. Dick has to clean all the **dirt** from his fingernails. **Dirty** is not clean.

do

Playing, jumping, skipping, working, laughing. People **do** all of these things. How many have you **done** to-day? Which **do** you like **doing** best?

dog

This **dog** is a furry friendly animal that barks. He might not like Dick Whittington's cat though!

doll

A **doll** is a toy that looks like a person. Do you like to play with **dolls**?

dollar

A **dollar** note is a special piece of paper used as money.

donkey

A **donkey** is a farm animal something like a horse. He has long ears and says, "Hee haw!"

door

Dick Whittington was fast asleep outside the **door** when Cook found him. A **door** is a way into a room, a house, a shed. Where else are **doors** used?

dot

A **dot** is a very small spot. The stars look like **dots** in the sky because they are so far away.

double

Double is twice. Hold three pencils in your hand. Hold three pencils in your other hand. Both hands together have two lots of three. You have **doubled** three and made six.

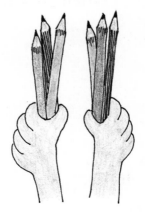

down

Alice went **down** the stairs to the
kitchen. It was on the bottom floor of the house.
To go **down** is to move from a high place to a lower
place.

draw

An artist can **draw** pictures with a
pencil or with charcoal. Do you like
drawing pictures with crayons?

drawer

Socks, hankies, pencils, string. Have
you got a **drawer** to keep things tidy?
Drawers usually come in chests. A
chest of **drawers** can hold lots of things.

dress

When Dick first saw Alice she was wearing a blue silk **dress**.

drink

You **drink** when you are thirsty. Water is a **drink**, so is tea.

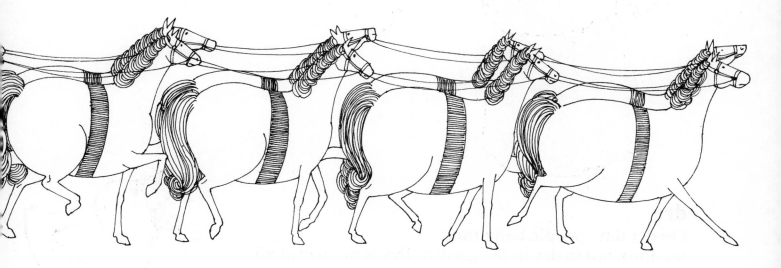

drive

Look at the rich people **driving** down
the streets in coaches pulled by horses.
The Lord Mayor of London **drove** to
Dick's wedding in a gilt coach with ten
white horses. These days people **drive**
cars instead to move from place to
place.

drop

Dick had to clean up every **drop** of
gravy that Cook spilt. She **dropped** it
because she was in a hurry.

dry
On **dry** days people hang their
washing out to dry in the garden. **Dry** is not wet at all.

duck
A **duck** is a bird that says, "Quack!"

duckling
A **duckling** is a baby duck.

dumb
Dick was so surprised that his cat had
made him a great fortune that he was
struck **dumb**. He could not speak.

dust
There was never a speck of **dust** on the
kitchen floor when Dick had cleaned
it. Even the very smallest piece of dirt
was swept up.

The Emperor's New Clothes

Once upon a time there lived an Emperor who was very vain. His only pleasure in life was that people should admire him in his fine clothes, and he spent a great deal of time changing his clothes and preening himself.

One day two men came to the court. They told the Emperor that they would like to weave him a fine new suit of clothes, better than any he had had before. The suit of clothes would be very expensive, and they would need to be paid in advance. Also, only those people who were clever and wise and well suited to their jobs would be able to see these fine clothes. To everyone else they would be invisible.

The Emperor was very excited about his new clothes. He sent his courtiers to see how quickly the weavers were making them. Of course, the courtiers did not want to admit that they could see nothing on the empty looms, so they pretended to admire the cloth.

The day of the Grand Procession came, when the new clothes were to be ready, and the Emperor was up early. He was horrified when his courtiers brought in his new clothes and he could not see them. He was afraid that if he said so everyone would think he was not suited to his job. So he said nothing and put on the clothes.

Out into the streets he went. He felt a little cool, but the weavers said that was because the cloth was so light and delicate.

All the people who had turned out to see the Emperor in his new clothes said "Ooh" and "Aah" and "Aren't they beautiful!" Nobody wanted to admit that he could see nothing.

Nobody, that is, except a little boy who didn't care if people thought he wasn't clever and wise and fit for his job. After all, he was too young to have a job.

As the Emperor moved down the street the little boy cried out, "He hasn't got anything on! The Emperor's got no clothes on!"

each

Each day the Emperor would change
his clothes about five times. He was so vain that he did it every day.

ear

You hear with your **ears**. You have one on each side of your head.
What else has **ears**?

early

On the day of the Grand Procession the
Emperor was up very **early**. He got up
as close to the start of the day as he
could. He didn't want to be late so he
was up **earlier** than usual.

east

The sun rises in the **east** every
morning. It sets in the west at night.

easy

The two cunning weavers found it was
very **easy** to make the Emperor believe
them. It was not hard because the
Emperor was so vain.

eat

We have to **eat** food to stay alive. But **eating** too much is bad for you.

egg

A baby bird hatches from an **egg**. Hens'
eggs are good to eat. You can cook
them in lots of different ways. Break
the shell of an **egg**. Inside is a yellow
yolk and a white albumen.

eight

Eight is 8.

either

"When they show me the new suit of clothes I shall **either** be able to see them
or I shall be unfit for my job," said the Emperor to himself. What happened?
Either means one or other of two things.

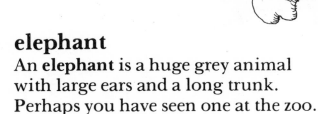

elephant
An **elephant** is a huge grey animal with large ears and a long trunk. Perhaps you have seen one at the zoo.

else
The weavers knew that the Emperor was very vain. How **else** could they have tricked him? In what other way could they have made him pay them a lot of money for doing nothing?

emu
An **emu** is a large Australian bird that doesn't fly. It can run very fast though.

end
"The Emperor's got no clothes on!" cried the little boy at the **end** of the story. The **end** comes last.

engine
A car needs an **engine** or it won't go! An **engine** is a machine.

enough
The Emperor did not feel quite warm **enough** in his new clothes. He wasn't as warm as he would like to be!

equal

Two and two **equal** four. Two and two are the same as four.

even

"The cloth is so **even** and smooth," said the courtiers. "It is not lumpy or rough at all."

ever

Have you **ever** heard of such a vain man as the Emperor? Have you heard of a person like him before? **Ever** means always, for all time.

every

Every person in the crowd said how wonderful the Emperor's new clothes were. All of them pretended they could see them. **Everybody** was tricked by the cunning weavers.

except

That is, everybody **except** the little boy was tricked. He was the only one who didn't care whether he was thought wise or not.

excuse

"**Excuse** me," said a man in the crowd. "I want to get through to see the Emperor."

eye

"I spy with my little **eye**." We can see with our **eyes**. What colour are yours?

Ff

The Frog Prince

Long ago a young Princess was very sad when she lost her golden ball. She had been playing with it in the Palace garden when she dropped it into the pond. As she sat there crying and feeling sorry for herself a voice croaked,

"What will you give me for fetching your ball?"

All the Princess could see was a green frog on a lily leaf. He wanted to sit at the Princess's table and eat from her plate and lie on her bed as a reward for fetching the ball. Of course, the Princess agreed and was overjoyed to get her golden ball back again. Then she ran all the way to the Palace, thinking the frog would get lost and go back to the pond.

Later, at supper in the Palace dining-room, the frog came in and reminded the Princess of what she had said. The King and Queen were very displeased with their daughter and said she must keep her promise.

So the Princess sat by with a sullen face while the ugly frog ate from her crystal plate and drank from her silver cup. Then he said he was tired and demanded to be carried upstairs to sleep on the Princess's silk pillow.

By the time the Princess was ready to climb into bed she had completely lost her temper with the frog. Instead of letting him sleep on her pillow she flung him out of the window on to the lawn below.

In a puff of smoke the frog disappeared and in his place stood a handsome prince! The Princess had broken a spell cast by an old witch, so she and the Frog Prince were married and rode away to live in the Prince's country.

face

Mouth, nose, eyes. They are all parts of
your **face**. Your **face** shows how you
feel. The Princess's **face** was sad when
she lost her golden ball.

fall

The Princess threw up her ball to
watch it **fall** through the air. It **fell**
down into the pond.

far

How **far** down did the ball go? Too **far**
for the Princess to reach.

fast

The Princess ran home **fast**. She ran
very quickly. She could run **faster** than
the frog.

fat

Don't eat too much. You might get **fat**!
The white part of meat is **fatty**.

father

Father is Daddy. The King is the Princess's **father**.

favourite

Your **favourite** story is the one you like best.

february

February is the second month of the year. It comes after January.

feel

How do you **feel** today? Are you cold, or hot, or tired, or happy?
A puppy **feels** warm and furry when you touch it. **Feel** also means to touch.

fence

There was a high **fence** all around the castle to keep people out. The Princess scrambled through the **fence** to get to the forest.

fight

Have you ever seen two dogs having a **fight**? They do it because they don't like each other.

fill

The Princess's eyes began to **fill** with tears when she lost her ball. The pond was so deep and **full** of water.

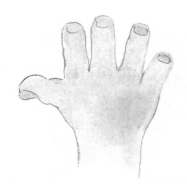

find

The frog said he would **find** the golden ball. He dived into the water and **found** it at the bottom of the pond.

finger

Each of your hands has four **fingers** and a thumb.

finish

The Princess would not **finish** her food after the frog had tasted it. **Finish** means end.

fine

The Queen's clothes were very **fine**. They were beautiful, and of the best quality.

fire

It is fun to cook dinner over a **fire** on the beach or in the garden. Does your house have a **fireplace** in it?

first

If you come **first** in a race you win it. One is the **first** number.

fish

There were **fish** swimming in the Palace pond. Do you like to eat **fish**?

fit

When you have new clothes they **fit** you well. They are not too tight or too loose.

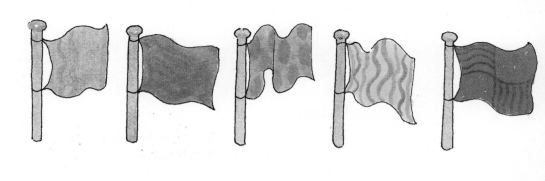

five
Five is 5.

fix
When a car breaks down it has to be taken to the garage. The mechanic will **fix** it. He mends it.

flag
A **flag** is made of cloth and hangs on a pole. It gives a sign. The first man on the moon put a **flag** there to show everyone he had been there.

flame
Fire! Fire! The **flames** are red and yellow and the smoke is thick and grey.

flat
The Princess's bed was smooth and **flat**. It was not lumpy.

floor
The Princess put the frog on the **floor** of her room. She did not want him on her bed.

flower

Which is your favourite **flower** — a rose, a camellia, a cornflower or . . ?

fly

A **fly** is a small insect with wings. It **flies** through the air. Aeroplanes and birds **fly** too.

foal

A **foal** is a baby horse.

follow

The frog has to **follow** the Princess back to the castle. He goes behind her.

foot

Your **foot** is at the end of your leg. **Feet** are for standing and walking on.

football

A **football** is a ball that is kicked with your foot. Do you like playing **football**?

forget
The Princess tried to **forget** her promise to the frog. She did not want to remember it.

fork
You use a **fork** to pick up your food. The **forks** in the palace are made of silver.

four
Four is 4.

fox
A **fox** is an animal with a red-brown coat and a bushy tail.

free
Air is **free**. It doesn't cost anything.

Friday
Friday is the sixth day of the week.

friend
A **friend** is a person you like to be with. You play with your **friends**.

frog
The **frog** in this story is very unusual. He turns into a prince!

from
The King and Queen heard the frog's voice. Where was it coming **from**? **From** behind the door.

front
The Princess ran off in **front** of the frog. She went first and he followed.

froth
Froth is foam. A milk-shake is **frothy**. So are the white waves on the beach.

fun
The Princess had lots of **fun** with her golden ball. She liked playing with it.

funny
Funny things make us laugh. What is the **funniest** thing you ever saw?

Goldilocks
and the Three Bears

A little girl called Goldilocks was playing in her garden when she took it into her head to go exploring. She went out through the garden gate and walked and walked until she came to a little house in the woods.

She knocked on the door but nobody answered, so she went in. On the table were three bowls of porridge. Goldilocks was hungry and couldn't resist eating the porridge. She climbed up on to a chair, but it was too big for her, and the big bowl of porridge was too hot. The second chair was also too big and the porridge too hot. The third bowl was smaller and the porridge was just right, but the chair was too small and the legs broke.

"I'm tired," thought Goldilocks and went off in search of somewhere to lie down. She found three beds and tried the big one first. But it was too big. The second one was too soft. The third one was the smallest, and it was just right. Goldilocks went to sleep.

A little while later, the three bears who lived in the house came back from their walk. At once the bears noticed that their chairs had been sat on and that Baby Bear's chair was broken and his porridge all gone!

They went upstairs.

Father Bear growled, "Someone's been lying on my bed."

Mother Bear said, "Someone's been lying on MY bed."

And Baby Bear said, "Someone's been lying on my bed — and she's STILL THERE!"

Just then Goldilocks woke up with a start. She was so frightened at seeing all those bears looking at her that she leapt up, ran down the stairs and out through the door. She didn't stop running until she reached home.

And she never went into a strange house on her own again.

game
Kicking a ball is a good **game**.

garden
You can grow fruit and vegetables in a **garden**. You can play there too. Goldilocks was naughty to go outside her **garden**.

gate
Look at Goldilocks going out through the garden **gate**.

get
The three bears will **get** a shock when they come home. Goldilocks has **got** into baby bear's bed and is **getting** a good sleep.

giant
There is a **giant** in this book, in the story of Jack and the Beanstalk. **Giants** are very large.

girl
Goldilocks is a **girl**. When she grows up she will be a woman.

give
The three bears **give** Goldilocks a fright when she wakes up. She wasn't expecting to see them there! It **gave** them a surprise to find her!

glass
Windows and bottles are made of **glass**. You can see through them. Father Bear wears **glasses** to help him see better.

glue
Glue is sticky. You can use it to stick things together.

62

go

Goldilocks **goes** slowly up the stairs. She is **going** to look for a comfy bed. She is so tired that she will **go** to sleep very quickly.

goal

A **goal** is made of two upright posts and a cross-bar. In some sports a **goal** also has a net. Everyone likes to score **goals**.

goat

A **goat** is an animal that eats plants and gives milk. Some **goats** have horns.

gold

Goldilocks got her name because her hair was the colour of **gold**. **Gold** costs a lot of money.

goldfish

Goldfish are kept in bowls or garden ponds. They get their name from their colour too.

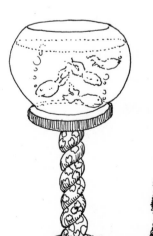

good

A **good** apple is nice to eat. You are **good** when you are doing the right thing and not being naughty.

goose

A **goose** is a bird that flies and swims. **Geese** are bigger than ducks and have longer necks.

gorilla

A **gorilla** is a very large ape. Goldilocks is not likely to meet a **gorilla** in the forest. **Gorillas** live in jungles in hot countries.

grain

A **grain** of sand is one very small piece of sand. Can you hold just one **grain** of sand or wheat on your finger?

grandmother

Your **grandmother** is the mother of your mother or father.

great

Father Bear is a **great** big bear. He is very big.

green

Green is the colour of grass. You can make the colour **green** by running blue and yellow together.

grey

Grey is the colour of an elephant.

ground

The **ground** is earth. You can stand on it, build things on it, travel across it and plant things in it.

grow

Baby Bear will **grow** and become a big bear like his father.

guess

The three bears cannot **guess** who has been in their house. They think it is a robber but they are wrong.

gum

The **gum** tree is a eucalyptus. Koalas live in **gum** trees.

Hh

Hansel and Gretel

There was once a poor woodcutter who had two children and a second wife. She was the children's stepmother.

Times were hard and there was not enough food for the four of them. The stepmother wanted the father to take Hansel and Gretel into the forest and leave them there. She thought there would be more food for her then.

The children overheard the stepmother's plans. When morning came the father took the children deep into the forest and left them there. But Hansel had dropped a trail of white pebbles all the way from the house, and he and Gretel were able to find their way home.

Next day, the same thing happened, but this time Hansel had dropped breadcrumbs on the path. The birds came and ate the crumbs. This time they were lost.

They wandered about and soon came to a very strange cottage. The walls were made of gingerbread, the roof of marzipan and it was filled with all sorts of other goodies. The old woman who lived there welcomed the children and asked them to stay.

After a week or two, Hansel and Gretel were quite plump, having eaten so much at the old woman's cottage. Then the old woman locked Hansel in the hen-house and told Gretel to heat up the oven. She was going to roast Hansel for her dinner!

Poor Gretel did as she was told, wondering how to rescue Hansel.

"Is the oven hot yet? Put your head in and see," shouted the old woman.

"I don't understand what you mean," said Gretel, who understood perfectly.

"Like this!" shrieked the witch, and put her head in the oven. Gretel gave her a hard push and then slammed the oven door shut.

She raced off to free Hansel from the hen-house, and the two of them were pleased as Punch to have outwitted the old witch.

They found lots of treasure in the cottage and managed to find their way back home. Their father was delighted to see them again, and the cruel stepmother had died. So the three were able to live happily together at last.

hair

Hair grows on your head. Gretel has brown **hair**, Hansel has short **hair**. What is yours like?

half

If you cut an apple in **half** you make two pieces. Each piece is the same size. There are two **halves** in a whole hour, or a whole loaf, or a whole stick. Two **halves** are always the same size.

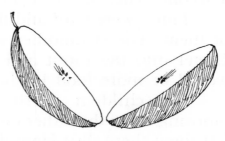

hand

Your **hand** is at the end of your arm. You use it to hold things. What else can you do with a **hand**?

handbag

A **handbag** is handy for carrying small things in. You can hold it in your hand.

handle

Gretel quickly fastened the oven door **handle** when she had pushed the old woman inside. **Handles** make things easy to hold. You can pick a saucepan up by the **handle**, or shut a door with a **handle**.

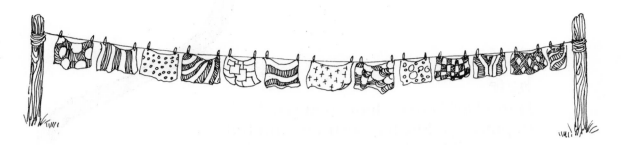

hang

It is good to **hang** the washing out on a fine day. It soon dries in the sun.

hanky

This is a short word for **handkerchief**. You blow your nose on a **hanky**.

happen

What will **happen** to Hansel and Gretel? Will the old woman eat them? If you know the story you know what **happens** to them.

hard

The floor of the cottage is made of **hard** stone. **Hard** can be the opposite of soft. The old woman made Gretel work very **hard** gathering wood for the fire.

hat

A big **hat**, a small **hat**, a wide **hat**, a tall **hat**. Which do you like best to wear on your head?

hate

Hansel and Gretel **hate** their cruel stepmother. She has been very unkind to them. They dislike her very much.

have

Have you seen a black cat like the old woman's? It **has** green eyes and a long smooth tail.

head

When the old woman put her **head** in the oven to test it, Gretel quickly pushed her right in.

hear

You **hear** sounds with your ears. Gretel **heard** Hansel calling from the hen-house.

heat

"You must test the **heat** of the oven before you put the goose in," said Gretel. **Heat** is how hot something is.

68

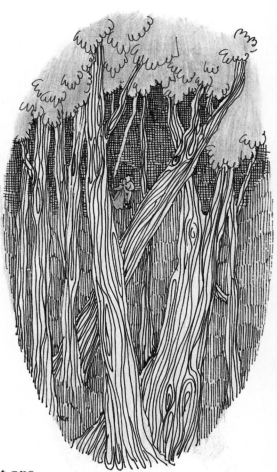

heavy

The old woman was quite **heavy** but Gretel pushed her very hard. You cannot lift or push something that is too **heavy**.

help

How are Hansel and Gretel going to get **help**? They are lost in the forest and there is no one to **help** them.

hen

A **hen** is a bird that lays eggs that are good to eat. Poor Hansel was locked in the **hen-house**.

here

Here is where you are. If you are **here** you are not anywhere else.

hide

Gretel had to **hide** behind the hen-house. She wanted to talk to Hansel. She didn't want the old woman to see her.

high

How **high** can you jump? The tops of the forest trees are very **high** up. The sky is even **higher**.

hill

A **hill** is a large mound on the ground.
It is not as big as a mountain.

hit

Do you ever **hit** a ball with a stick? You do if you play cricket!

hold

Hansel's pockets are big enough to
hold lots of white pebbles. As he
walked through the forest he **held** some
in his hand and dropped them on the
ground.

hole

A **hole** is a space with air in it. You can
dig a **hole** in the ground, or poke a
hole in paper, or cut a **hole** in material.
Where else can you have **holes**?

holiday

A **holiday** is a time free from work when everybody can do what he or she likes.
Lots of people go to the beach for their **holidays**.

home

Hansel and Gretel found their way
home by following the trail of pebbles.
Home is where you live. Animals have
homes too.

hop
Frogs **hop**. You can **hop** if you try to walk on one foot.

hope
Hansel and Gretel **hope** that they are not going to be lost in the forest for ever. They want to find somewhere to live.

horse
A **horse** is a large animal with hooves and a long tail. He is strong and can carry people.

hot
In the summer when the sun is out it is very **hot**. **Hot** is the opposite of cold.

hour
When the large hand on a clock has moved round once, one **hour** has passed. There are twenty-four **hours** in a day.

house
The old woman lives in a **house** made of gingerbread and chocolate and other yummy things.

how
"**How** did you get back home?" That's what the wicked stepmother thought when she saw Hansel and Gretel on the doorstep.

hundred
One **hundred** is a big number. Put ten lots of ten beads, or bricks, or biscuits, or balloons, together. You will have a **hundred**.

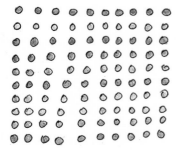

hungry
Hansel and Gretel were very **hungry** after their long walk. They had not had anything to eat since breakfast.

hurry
"**Hurry** up! Walk very quickly," said Hansel to Gretel when they were near the old woman's cottage.

hurt
The heat of the oven was beginning to **hurt** the old woman. It was very hot and gave her a pain in her arm.

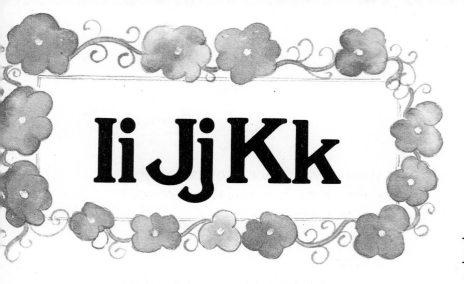

Ii Jj Kk

Jack and the Beanstalk

Once upon a time there was a boy called Jack who lived with his widowed mother. They were very poor and the only thing they had to sell was a thin white cow. Instead of selling the cow in the market Jack exchanged it for five magic beans.

His mother was furious. "No cow, no money, just five stupid beans!" she screamed, and flung the beans out of the window.

Next morning the beans had sprouted — grown right up to the sky! Jack started climbing up the beanstalk. He climbed and climbed to the sky. Not far away he could see a castle.

He approached boldly and knocked on the door. A large woman answered. Seeing a hungry boy she warned Jack that her husband was a Giant who was very fond of boys for supper and that he'd better keep well hidden.

Just then the Giant's footsteps started to shake the ground. The woman hid Jack in the cupboard and set about cooking the Giant's supper. The Giant sniffed and snuffed and roared,

"Fe Fi Fo Fum, I smell the blood of an Englishman.
Be he alive or be he dead
I'll grind his bones to make my bread!"

But the wife said, "Nonsense," and gave him his supper.

Afterwards, the Giant started counting his money. Then he fell asleep and Jack darted nimbly out of the cupboard, took two bags of gold and ran back to the beanstalk.

A week later Jack thought he would visit the Giant again, and see what else he could take. Again the Giant's wife fed him and hid him, this time in the washtub. He watched the Giant eat his supper and play with his golden bags until he fell asleep.

Jack jumped out of the washtub and stole the golden harp, and raced back to the beanstalk. But this time the Giant saw him and was right behind him.

When he reached his garden, Jack called for his mother to bring the axe. He managed to cut down the beanstalk and the Giant crashed to the ground and lay still.

And Jack and his mother were never hungry again.

ice

Ice is frozen water. **Ice-blocks** and **ice-cream** are frozen too and they are cool to eat on hot days.

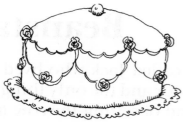

icing

What a pretty cake, covered in **icing**. The **icing** is made of sugar and water and colouring. It is very sweet.

idea

After Jack had stolen the Giant's gold coins he sat down and thought. Then he said, "I've had an **idea**! If I go up the beanstalk again I might be able to bring back some more treasure."

if

The Giant would have eaten Jack **if** he had found him.

ink

Ink is the coloured liquid inside pens. It makes a mark on the paper when you write.

inside

From **inside** the cupboard, looking out, Jack could see the Giant counting his money. Jack was peeping through a crack in the door.

instead

Jack's mother was very cross when she
found that Jack had sold the cow for
five beans **instead** of money.

into

The Giant's wife popped Jack **into** the
cupboard to hide him when the Giant
came home.

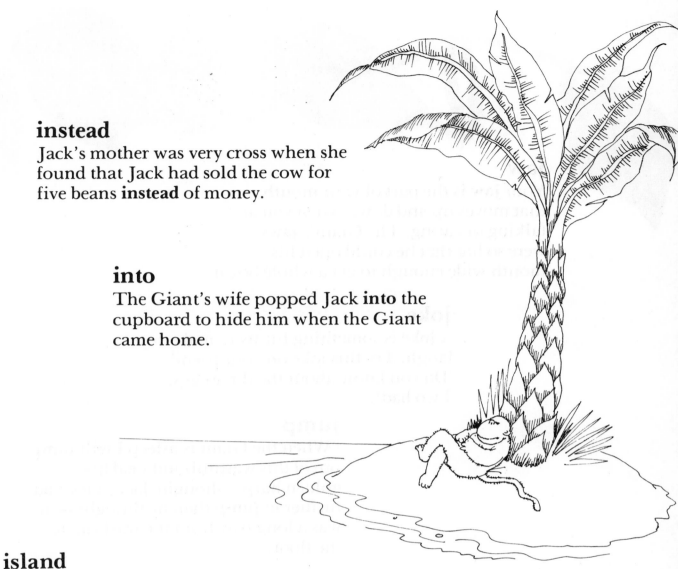

island

An **island** is a piece of land with water
all around it. **Islands** can be big or small. Do you live on an **island**?

jacket

Jack and his mother were so poor that
Jack's **jacket** was very old and tattered. A **jacket** is a short coat.

January

January is the first month of the year.

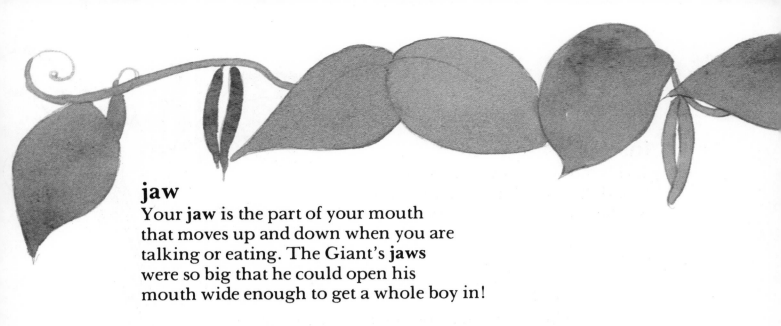

jaw

Your **jaw** is the part of your mouth
that moves up and down when you are
talking or eating. The Giant's **jaws**
were so big that he could open his
mouth wide enough to get a whole boy in!

joke

A **joke** is something funny to make you
laugh. Try this joke on your friends.
'Do you know about the three eggs?
Two bad!'

jump

"When the Giant is asleep I will **jump**
out of this washtub and steal his
golden harp," thought Jack. Jack had
further to **jump** than he thought — it
was a long way from the washtub to
the floor.

jumper

The Giant was wearing a rough
woolly **jumper** to keep him warm up
there in the sky.

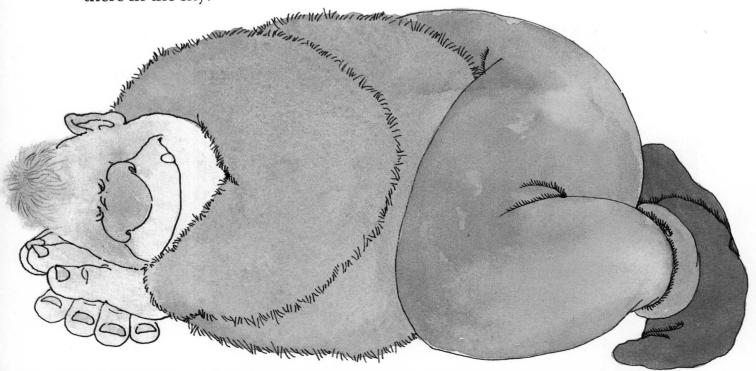

July

July is the seventh month of the year. It comes after June.

June

June is the sixth month of the year. It comes after May.

jungle

A **jungle**, in hot, wet lands, is a dark place so full of trees and creepers that only a little light comes through the leaves. Jack's beanstalk must have looked like a **jungle** — it had so many branches and enormous leaves.

just

"I must go up the beanstalk **just** one more time," said Jack to himself. "I shall not go up any more after that." To be **just** is to be fair. A judge must give a **just** decision when a person is tried in court. He must decide what is right.

kangaroo

A **kangaroo** is a large Australian animal that hops and carries her babies in her pouch.

keep

"Take the cow to market, Jack. We cannot **keep** her now. We must get rid of her, to get some money," said Jack's mother.

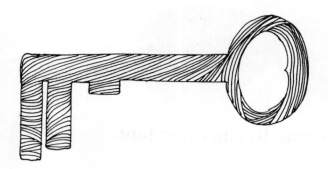

key

A **key** fits in a lock through a **keyhole**. You can lock a door or a suitcase with it. The Giant must have had a very big **key** for his door!

kick

You **kick** a ball with your foot.

kid

A **kid** is a baby goat.

kill

The Giant would like to **kill** Jack so that he can cook him and have him for supper. But Jack doesn't want to be **killed**. He wants to stay alive.

kind

The Giant's wife was **kind** to Jack. She was his friend. She gave him some food and hid him in the cupboard when the Giant came home.

kindergarten

Kindergarten is a school for young children.

king

A **king** is the ruler of a country. He wears a crown and sits on a throne. There are often **kings** (and queens) in fairy stories. Is there a **king** in Jack and the Beanstalk?

kitchen

The Giant's wife let Jack help her in the **kitchen** where she was cooking the Giant's supper.

kite

A **kite** is made of paper and flies high in the air.
Kites are brightly coloured. You have to hold on to the string or the **kite** will fly away for ever.

kitten

A **kitten** is a baby cat.

knife

Watch out! That **knife** is sharp! But it is not sharp enough to cut down the beanstalk. Jack's mother will have to use the axe!

knock

"**Knock, knock!**" Jack's fist rapped on the big wooden door of the Giant's castle. He was too short to reach the **knocker**.

knot

Jack tied the rope around the cow's head and fastened the ends with a **knot**, so that it would not come undone.

know

"Do you **know** how many beans make five?" the old woman asked Jack. "Yes, I can show you how many make five," said Jack.

koala

A **koala** is a small furry Australian animal. It lives in gum trees.

Ll

The Brave Little Tailor

There was once a little tailor who killed seven flies with one stroke. He made himself a belt and stitched *seven at one stroke* across it and set off to look for adventure.

After a while he met a giant and asked him if they should travel together. The giant was very impressed by the words on the tailor's belt, and agreed to walk with him. The giant took the tailor to the cave where he lived with two other giants. They were so big and fierce that the little tailor ran all the way to the nearest town. He wearily lay down by the palace gates to sleep.

The King heard about the tailor and his belt which said *seven at one stroke* and decided that he must be a hero. He sent for the tailor and asked him to rid his country of the three giants who robbed and killed the people.

The tailor rode off with a hundred knights to search for the giants. He carried a bundle of hay on his horse. When he reached the mountain where the giants lived he told the knights to wait. He climbed the mountain with his bundle of hay and stuffed it into the giants' chimney to make it smoke. When they came home he heard them coughing and sneezing in the smoke-filled cave. The giants staggered out to search for a better cave. The little tailor slipped in and dragged their great knives all the way down the mountain to the knights.

Everyone said the tailor was a hero. They all thought he had killed the giants, and the King let him marry the Princess.

But one day the King found out that the tailor was really a tailor and not a hero. He ordered seven guards to keep watch outside his bedroom door. The Princess was worried and told the tailor of her father's plan.

The tailor pretended to talk in his sleep, and said, "I killed seven at one stroke. One stroke will kill the seven who wait outside my door."

So the guards hurried away and told the King that the tailor was indeed a hero.

lady

A **lady** is a woman. A mother is a **lady**. Girls grow up to be **ladies**.

lamb

A **lamb** is a baby sheep.

last

The tailor rode off with a hundred knights to look for the giants. The **last** knight rode at the end of the line.

late

When you are **late** for dinner you get there after everybody else. You arrive **later** than you should.

lawn

The **lawn** in the palace garden was smooth and green. A **lawn** is made of grass which is cut and watered carefully so that it looks and feels good.

lead

The tailor will **lead** the knights to the giants' cave. He goes in front. He is the **leader**.

leaf

A **leaf** grows on a plant. In autumn some of the **leaves** turn brown and fall on the ground.

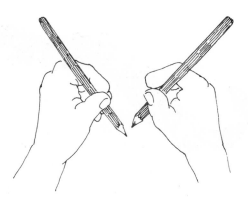

leave

"I shall **leave** this town, go away in search of adventure," said the little tailor.

left

Do you write with your **left** hand or your right hand?

leg

The tailor had walked so far that his **legs** were very tired.

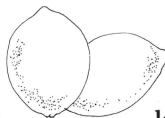

lemon

A **lemon** is a yellow fruit with thick skin. The juice is very bitter.

lend

"**Lend** me a pony," said the little tailor to the king. "Let me borrow it for a while."

leopard

A **leopard** is a big fierce animal. It is a bit like a tiger, with spots instead of stripes.

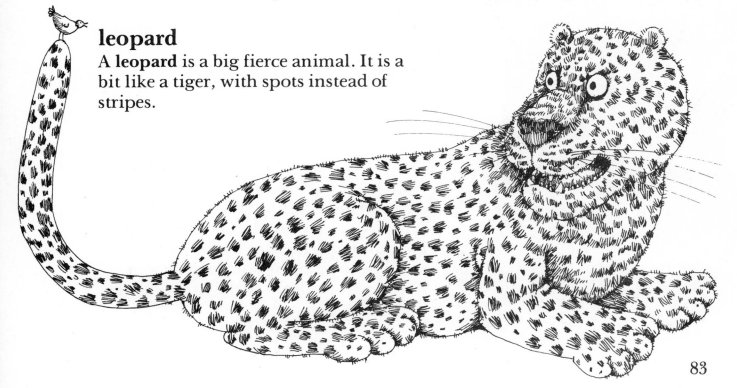

SEVEN AT ONE STROKE

let

"We will **let** you kill the giants," said the king to the little tailor. "You are allowed to do it."

letter

The little tailor sewed each **letter** on to his belt. The **letters** made the words "Seven at One Stroke". There are twenty-six **letters** in the alphabet.

lettuce

A **lettuce** is a green and leafy vegetable. It is good to eat in salads. (Rabbits like it too.)

library

A **library** is a room or building holding books. Do you borrow books from a **library**?

lift

The giants' huge knives were so heavy that the tailor could not **lift** them. He had to drag them instead. To **lift** is to raise.

light

The sun gives **light**. If there is no **light** it is very hard to see. In the dark you have to switch on the electric **light** to see. The little tailor saw the giants in the cave by the **light** of the fire.

like

The giant's knife is **like** a great big sword to the brave little tailor. The tailor does not **like** the look of it at all — it is so big!

line

The knights rode out of the palace courtyard in a long **line**. They rode one behind the other.

lion

A **lion** is a large fierce animal from the cat family. **Lion** cubs look very cuddly but they have long claws.

listen

The tailor stuffed his hay down the giants' chimney. "Now I will wait and **listen** for the noise that will show they have come home," he said.

little

Little is small, like the brave **little** tailor.

live

Where do you **live**? In a house, or a flat, a boat or a caravan? The giants **live** in a cave.

lock

You can **lock** a door or a suitcase with a key. Then only the person with the key can **unlock** it.

long

The little tailor dragged the giants' knives down the **long** mountain path. It was quite a **long** time before he reached the knights again.

look

"**Look**!" said the knights. "The little tailor has killed three giants! He **looks** like a hero!"

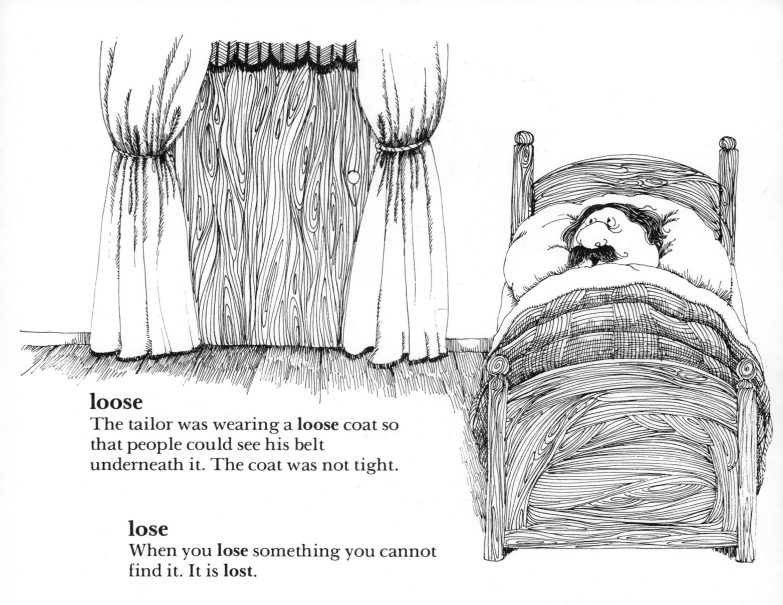

loose

The tailor was wearing a **loose** coat so that people could see his belt underneath it. The coat was not tight.

lose

When you **lose** something you cannot find it. It is **lost**.

loud

The little tailor wanted the guards to hear him. He said out **loud**, noisily, "I killed seven at one stroke. One stroke will kill the seven who wait outside my door."

love

Mummy and Daddy **love** you and they **love** each other too. To **love** is to like very much.

lovely

The Princess was so **lovely** that the little tailor wanted to marry her. She was very beautiful.

lucky

The little tailor was **lucky** because the seven guards could hear what he said when he pretended to be asleep. **Luck** is good fortune.

lunch

Twelve o'clock is time for **lunch**. Would you like a sandwich to eat?

Mm

Rumplestiltskin

Once upon a time there was a miller's daughter who was very sad. Her father had told the King that she could spin straw into gold, and now here she was, locked in a big room full of straw, and expected to turn it into gold by morning!

The poor girl sat crying. She wondered what was to become of her — when the door opened and a strange little man came in.

He told the miller's daughter that he would spin the straw into gold in return for her necklace.

In the morning the King was delighted at the sight of all the gold and told the girl to do the same thing the following night.

Once again the little man appeared, and in return for the girl's ring, spun the straw into gold.

The King told the miller's daughter to spin gold a third time, and then she would be his wife. This time she had nothing left to give the little man, so he said he would have her first child when she became Queen.

A year passed and the Queen had a beautiful baby. She had forgotten the little man so was surprised when he appeared and demanded that she keep her promise. The Queen was horrified. She offered him all her riches. But he only wanted the child.

The Queen was so upset that the little man said he would give her three days in which to find out his name. If she hadn't guessed it by then the child would be his.

The Queen sent out a messenger to find out as many different names as he could, but when the little man returned next day he said 'No' to all of them.

The messenger went out again and as he was riding through the wood, he saw a little man dancing round a fire singing:

"Happily I'll dance and sing, Tomorrow I'll a baby bring.
Little does the young Queen dream
Rumpelstiltskin is my name!"

When the strange little man came again to the Palace the Queen drew a deep breath and said,

"Is your name Rumpelstiltskin?"

The little man screamed with rage and stamped his foot so hard that it went right through the floorboard. Then he hobbled away and has never been heard of since.

magic
Rumpelstiltskin could spin straw into gold as if by **magic**. Fairy stories have marvellous **magic** people in them. They can do amazing things.

magician
A **magician** does magic tricks. He can pull white rabbits from hats, or turn black cats into white mice, or . . . Can you tell about a **magician** you know?

make
Rumpelstiltskin said he would **make** the straw into gold so that the miller's daughter would not have to die. By morning he had **made** all the straw in the room into gold.

man
A **man** is a grown-up boy. Daddies and Uncles are **men**.

many
By the end of the third night Rumpelstiltskin had turned so **many** bales of straw into gold that the King said, "That is enough gold for me now."

marble

Marble is a kind of stone. The colour is streaky like the **marbles** you play with. Palaces are sometimes built of **marble**.

March

March is the third month of the year. It comes after February.

mast

A **mast** is a tall pole on a boat. The sails are fastened to the **mast**.

match

Rumpelstiltskin's two boots **match** each other. They look the same.

matter

The miller's daughter was in despair at the thought of making straw into gold. "What is the **matter**? What's wrong?" asked Rumpelstiltskin.

May

May is the fifth month of the year. It comes before June.

mean

When the miller's daughter said Rumpelstiltskin could have her first child, did she **mean** it? Did she just say it because she didn't want to die? **Mean** also **means** unkind.

meat

Meat is the flesh of an animal. Lamb chops and roast beef and sausages are all **meat**.

melon

A **melon** is a delicious fruit with seeds inside. It grows on a vine.

melt

If you warm ice it will **melt** and become water. Ice-cream **melts** on hot days.

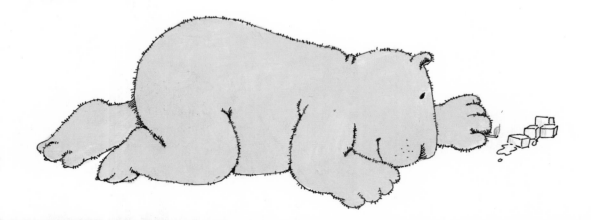

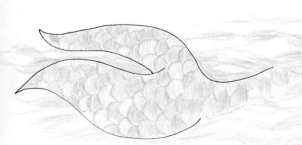

mermaid

Have you ever seen a **mermaid**? A **mermaid** looks like a girl with a fish's tail. **Mermaids** and mermen are magic people.

mess

What a **mess** Rumpelstiltskin looks! His beard is long and tangled and his clothes are untidy.

microphone

A **microphone** makes sounds louder. Singers use **microphones** on stage so that everyone can hear their voices.

middle

The Queen's messenger saw Rumpelstiltskin dancing round a fire in the **middle** of the woods. There were trees all around him and he thought no one would see him. What happened?

milk

We drink the **milk** that comes from cows. Babies drink **milk** from their mothers.

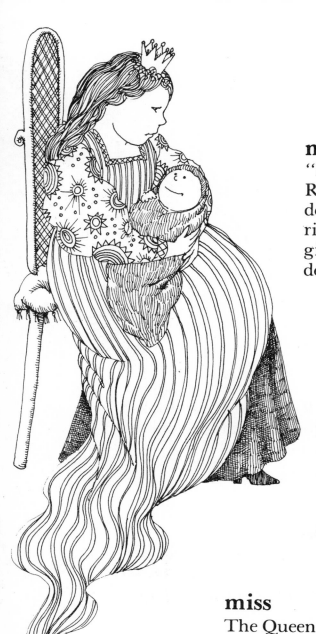

mind

"Please do not ask for my baby, Rumpelstiltskin," said the Queen. "I do not **mind** if I have to give you all the riches of my kingdom, but I do **mind** giving you my baby. I do not want to do it."

mine

"This gold is **mine**," said the King. "It belongs to me. I am rich!"

minute

A **minute** is sixty seconds. Count to sixty slowly and you will have counted for one **minute**.

miss

The Queen would **miss** her baby if she had to give it to Rumpelstiltskin. She would be lonely without it.

mixture

Bread is made from a **mixture** of flour and water and yeast. They are beaten together and kneaded and baked.

Monday

Monday is the second day of the week. It comes after Sunday.

money

Money is what we use to buy things with. **Money** is usually notes or coins.

monkey

A **monkey** is an animal with four legs and a long tail. He is very good at swinging in the trees. Have you seen a **monkey** at the zoo?

monster

Rumpelstiltskin looked rather like a **monster** to the Queen. He was so wrinkled and strange-looking. **Monsters** come in all shapes and sizes. They do not look quite like any other people or animals.

moon

Look up in the sky at night and you will see the **moon**. The **moon** rotates around the earth. It is a satellite.

more

"I need **more** gold," said the King. "I haven't got enough yet. Spin all this straw into gold by morning."

morning

Morning comes between night and noon.
The sun rises in the **morning**.

mother

Mother is Mummy. Do you think
Rumpelstiltskin had a **mother**, or was he made by magic?

motor

A car has a **motor**. It is a machine that
makes a car move. Think of some other
things with **motors**.

mouse

A **mouse** is a very small animal with a
long tail. There are lots of different kinds of **mice**.

mouth

Your **mouth** is in your face. You put food into it and speak through it.

move

The King would not allow the miller's
daughter to **move** from her room all
night. She had to stay there and spin
the straw into gold.

mud

Mud is very wet soil. It is slimy and dark and messy.

mushroom

A **mushroom** is a small plant like a fat umbrella. **Mushrooms** are good to eat but
toadstools are not. Some toadstools look like **mushrooms**.

Nn

Snow White
and the Seven Dwarfs

Once upon a time there was a beautiful Queen who became very jealous when her magic mirror told her,

"Lady Queen, you are still fair,
But none to Snow White can compare!"

She sent for a huntsman and told him to take Snow White deep into the forest and kill her. The huntsman could not bear to kill the girl. He left her in the forest and told her never to return to the Palace.

Snow White wandered along and came at last to a small cottage. Inside there were seven places set at a table and seven beds to lie on. Snow White took a nibble from each plate and then went to sleep on one of the beds.

When night fell, the Seven Dwarfs, who lived in the cottage, returned from their work. They heard Snow White's story and said she could live with them.

For a while life was happy, but then the Queen found out from her magic mirror that Snow White was still alive. She disguised herself as an old woman and walked to the cottage. The dwarfs were at work and the wicked Queen found it very easy to trick Snow White into taking first some lace, then a poisoned comb and finally a piece of poisoned apple.

In the evening the dwarfs came home and found Snow White on the floor. They thought she was dead and were very sad. She looked so beautiful that they made her a glass coffin with her name on it, and carried her in it to the hillside.

Several years later a Prince came riding by. He thought Snow White so beautiful that he kissed her; and as he did so the piece of poisoned apple fell from her mouth and she awoke.

Naturally, because Snow White was really a Princess, she and the Prince were married. The wicked Queen, on hearing of the wedding from her magic mirror was seized with a fit of blind rage, and her heart burst.

Snow White and her Prince lived happily ever after.

nail
The magic mirror on the wall hung from a **nail**. A **nail** is like a big heavy pin.

name
How did Snow White get her **name**? She was **named** Snow White because her skin was as white as snow.

naughty
If you have been **naughty**, you have done something wrong.

near
When the prince came **near** the glass case he saw Snow White lying in it. He rode even **nearer** and when he was very close to her he could see how beautiful she was.

neck
Your **neck** is between your head and your shoulders. It holds your head up.

need
The Seven Dwarfs did not wake Snow White when they saw her asleep in their cottage. They knew she would **need** a good rest. She had to have a sleep after walking so far.

nest
A bird lives in a **nest**. **Nests** are usually made from twigs and leaves, and birds lay their eggs in them.

never

The huntsman told Snow White,
"Run away and **never** return. Do not
ever come back or you will be killed."

new

The wicked Queen, dressed as an old
woman, offered Snow White the **new**
comb. It was not old. Nobody had used
it before.

next

The **next** thing the Queen gave Snow
White was a poisoned apple. She gave
her that after the new comb.

nice

Snow White thought the Seven Dwarfs were very **nice**. She liked them.

night

At **night** the sun has set and it is dark.
You can see the moon and stars at night.

nine

Nine is 9. There were
seven dwarfs. Two
more would make
nine.

nobody

Snow White knocked on the cottage
door but there was **nobody** there to open it. Where were the dwarfs?

noise

A **noise** is a sound. What **noises** can
you hear now? Do you ever make too much **noise**?

none

None is not one or not any. "Are there any cakes left?" asked Happy at tea-time. "No, there are **none** left," replied Snow White.

nose

Your **nose** sticks out from your face.
You breathe through it and smell through it.

nothing

"Is there anything we can do to help Snow White?" asked Sleepy. "No, there is **nothing**. We can't do anything," said Grumpy.

November

November is the eleventh month of the year. It comes before December.

now

What are you doing **now**, at this moment? You are reading this book, of course!

number

Four is a **number**. So is two, and six and five and ... You think of some more **numbers**.

nut

Walnuts, peanuts, brazil nuts, almonds. Which kind of **nut** do you like best? **Nuts** are seeds and good to eat.

Oo

Puss in Boots

There was once a Miller's son whose only possession in the world was a cat. One day he asked the cat what he could do to make his living and to his surprise the cat replied:

"Do as I say, Master, and you will be rich."

The cat was no ordinary creature so the young man did as he was told and found the cat a pair of strong boots and a sack.

Puss marched off and caught two rabbits in his sack. He took them to the Palace and told the King they were a present from his master, the Marquis of Carabas. The King was very pleased.

A few days later, Puss told his master to take his clothes off and bathe in the river. Puss took the clothes and hid them in a ditch. As he did so the King's carriage came down the road.

Puss ran out, shouting for help for his drowning master. He said that the Marquis of Carabas had been robbed of all his fine clothes and jewels and thrown in the river. The King's servants rescued the Miller's son and dressed him in some of the King's clothes. The King invited him to ride in the royal carriage.

Puss ran ahead and soon came to some people working in the fields. He told them that they must say these lands belonged to the Marquis of Carabas, or be chopped into small pieces.

Of course, the King stopped to admire the fine fields and asked to whom they belonged.

"To the Marquis of Carabas, Sire," was the reply.

Meanwhile Puss had reached the castle of a very cruel and fierce Ogre, who could turn himself into anything he wanted.

Puss-in-Boots went striding in and told the Ogre that he had heard wonderful stories about him and wondered if they were true.

"Oh sir, you are so mighty and powerful, can you really change yourself into something as small as a mouse?"

"I'll show you," roared the Ogre, and changed himself into a mouse, which Puss caught and ate in a trice.

When the King arrived at the castle, all the servants knew that they had a new master, the Marquis of Carabas. The King was most impressed by the splendour of the place and gave his daughter in marriage to the Miller's son.

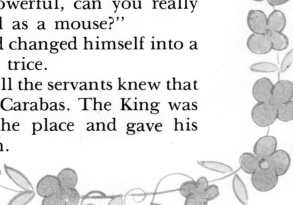

o'clock
Twelve **o'clock** is lunch-time. Five **o'clock** is tea-time. What time does your clock say?

October
October is the tenth month of the year. It comes after September.

off
"Take your clothes **off**, master, and jump in the river," said Puss. "You cannot swim with them on."

old
An **old** tree is not young. It has been living for a long time.

on
Where are you sitting? **On** a chair? **On** the floor? **On** a swing?

once
Once is one time. Puss-in-Boots tricked the ogre **once**. He only needed to do it one time to get rid of him.

one
One is 1.

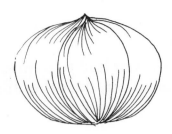

onion
An **onion** is a vegetable with a strong smell that makes your eyes water.

only
"If you want to make a fortune, master, you **only** have to do as I say," said Puss. "That is all you need to do."

open
"**Open** the carriage door," cried the King. "Let the Marquis of Carabas get in and ride with us."

orange
An **orange** is a juicy fruit. It is **orange** in colour.

order
"I **order** all of you to say that these lands belong to the Marquis of Carabas," said Puss to the Ogre's servants. "You must do it."

other

Puss's master had two brothers. One had black hair, the **other** had brown hair.

out

"I cannot get **out** of the water, Your Majesty," said Puss's master. **Out** is not in.

over

Pick up a book, or a leaf, or a pencil, or anything. Turn it **over** and look at the part that was underneath. Now look out of the window. Can you see **over** the top of the houses or trees?

own

"Now you have a castle of your **own** Master," purred Puss. "It belongs to you."

The Pied Piper of Hamelin

Six hundred years ago in the German city of Hamelin, a very strange thing happened.

Rats! They were everywhere — scratching and eating and spoiling, even biting babies in cradles. The Mayor and Aldermen had no idea what to do about them. As they sat in the Town Hall, wondering, a man in a red and yellow coat, carrying a pipe, came in. He promised to get rid of the rats for a thousand guilders.

"*Fifty* thousand!" shouted the Mayor and Aldermen, delighted.

The Piper went into the street, playing his pipe. All the rats tumbled out of the houses and followed him...all the way to the river, where they jumped in and were never seen again.

Then the Pied Piper asked for his thousand guilders. The Mayor knew the rats were drowned. He offered the Piper fifty.

The Piper said nothing. He began to play his pipe again and all at once children came running and dancing and clapping from the houses, following the Piper.

None of the grown-ups of Hamelin could move. They just had to stand and watch as all the children ran past them following the Piper. They thought that when the Piper reached the mountain he would turn back.

But no! At the foot of the mountain a door opened and the Pied Piper and the children went in. All except a lame boy who couldn't keep up. He was the only child left in the city of Hamelin.

pack

The people of Hamelin had to **pack** all their food into strong boxes so that the rats could not eat it. They put together as much as they could in the boxes. Do you **pack** your clothes in a suitcase when you go on holiday?

packet

Here is a **packet** of raisins that a rat has found!

page

These words are written on a **page** in this book. How many **pages** are in the book altogether?

paint

Artists **paint** pictures with coloured **paint** and brushes. Do you like **painting**?

panda

A Giant **Panda** is a large black and white animal. Have you seen a photo of a **Panda** at the zoo?

pant

Do you **pant** when you have been running about? **Panting** is breathing heavily.

paper

The pages of this book are made of **paper**. What else is?

pardon

To **pardon** is to forgive. The Pied Piper did not **pardon** the Mayor and Aldermen for breaking their promise. What did he do?

park

A **park** is a grassy place made especially for people to have fun in. Some **parks** have swings and roundabouts in them. Often a **park** is bushland. A car **park** is a place to leave cars.

parrot

A **parrot** is a brightly coloured bird
that can sometimes be taught to speak.

part

Which **part** of the Pied Piper's clothes
do you like best? The red **part** or the
yellow **part**?

party

A **party** is a group of people who get
together to have fun, or for other
things. Birthday **parties** are best. There
are candles to blow out on the cake!

pass

The children **pass** their parents who
cannot move. They run by them. They
run **past** the little lame boy. They
overtake him. The Piper leads them
over the **pass**, a narrow way, between
the mountains, and in through the big
wooden door.

patch

One little boy has a **patch** on his coat.
His mother has sewn it on to cover a
hole.

path

The Piper led the children on a winding **path** up the mountain.

pattern

Have a look at the Piper's scarf with its stripy **pattern**. What kind of a **pattern** is there on his sleeves?

paw

A **paw** is an animal's foot. Rats have four **paws**. What else does?

pawpaw

A **pawpaw** is a large yellow fruit with lots of black seeds inside it. It grows in hot climates.

pay

"If I get rid of the rats will you **pay** me one thousand guilders?" asked the Piper. "We'll give you *fifty* thousand," said the Mayor and Aldermen together.

pea

A **pea** is a small round green vegetable that grows in a pod.

peach

A **peach** is a round, sweet, summer fruit with a skin like velvet. It has a large stone inside it.

peanut

A **peanut** grows in a shell on roots underground. Monkeys like **peanuts**. Do you?

pear

A **pear** is an autumn fruit rather like an apple.

pen

A **pen** is for writing. It has ink inside it.

pencil

A **pencil** is for writing too. It has wood on the outside.

people

The **people** of Hamelin hated the rats. All the grown ups and the children were pleased to see them go.

person

You are a **person**. Everyone is a **person**.

pet

Do you have a **pet**? A **pet** is an animal that you keep because you like it.

photograph

A **photograph** is a picture taken with a camera.

piano

A **piano** is a large musical instrument. It has a keyboard and pedals.

pick

The Piper looked as though he could not wait to **pick** up his pipe and start playing. He knew that if he **picked** the right tune the rats would follow him. What happened when he started playing?

picnic

A **picnic** is a meal eaten out of doors.
Where is your favourite place for a **picnic**?

picture

On this page the artist has drawn a
picture of a pig with some cakes.

pie

A **pie** has pastry on the outside and
meat or apples or some other nice food
inside.

piece

A greedy rat has eaten a very large **piece**
of this apple pie!

pig

A **pig** is a farm animal with a curly
tail. **Pig** meat is called pork or ham or
bacon.

pile

What a large **pile** of cakes! They are
piled up one on top of the other. If the
rats find it the **pile** won't be big much
longer!

pin

A **pin** is a strong thin piece of wire
with one sharp end and one blunt end.

pineapple

A **pineapple** is a delicious tropical fruit
with a prickly skin.

pink

Pink is the colour of the pirate's shirt.

pirate

A **pirate** is a robber who steals things from ships.

place

Hamelin must have been a very quiet
place when all the children had left.
The Piper had taken them to a new
place. Where was it?

plastic

Biro tops, ice-cream containers, rulers,
telephones — all these things are made
of different kinds of **plastic**. Find some
more.

plate
A **plate** is for putting food on. It can be made from china, metal, glass or wood.

platypus
A **platypus** is a small brown Australian animal that lives in rivers.

play
"I can **play** a tune on my pipe that will make any living creature follow me," said the Piper. The children all thought it would be fun to dance and **play** behind the Piper. You **play** games for fun.

please
"**Please** could I have my thousand guilders?" asked the Piper politely.

plum
A **plum** is a purple fruit with a stone inside.

plus

Plus means and. It can be written like this +. One **plus** one makes two.

pocket

Oh dear! There is a rat coming out of this little boy's **pocket**!

point

The **point** of a pencil or a knife is the sharp end. Can you **point** to the spotted shirt on this page with your finger?

poke

To **poke** is to push a point into something. Go outside and **poke** the soil with a stick.

policeman

A **policeman** keeps law and order. He wears a special uniform.

poor

Many children in the world are so **poor** that they do not have enough to eat or drink. **Poor** means to be in want.

port

A **port** is where ships come in and tie up.

poster

A **poster** is a big picture to put on the wall.

potato

A **potato** is a vegetable that grows underground.

pour

When the Piper played the rats began to **pour** out of the houses. They streamed out the way water **pours** from a jug.

present

A **present** is a gift. You give **presents** to people you like at Christmas and on birthdays.

116

Little Red Riding Hood

Once upon a time there was a little girl who was sent to visit her Grandmother at the other side of the wood. She was called Red Riding Hood because she had a new red coat with a large hood.

Although little Red Riding Hood had been TOLD not to stray from the path, she saw so many pretty flowers to pick that she couldn't help herself. Along came a large grey Wolf who asked her where she was going. He seemed such a friendly Wolf that Red Riding Hood told him.

When she reached Grandmother's house Red Riding Hood was surprised to see her Grandmother sitting up in bed, not looking quite her usual self. She went closer and said in surprise,

"O Grandmother, what great ears you have!"

"All the better to hear you with, my dear," replied the Wolf, for indeed it was the Wolf.

"O Grandmother, what great eyes you have!"

"All the better to see you with, my dear."

"O Grandmother, what great TEETH you have!" exclaimed Red Riding Hood, astonished. And the Wolf leapt out of bed, all ready to eat her up. But just then a wasp flew in and stung the Wolf on the nose. He let out a great howl, there was a 'Hisht' sound and he fell back, dead.

Red Riding Hood turned and saw the Green Archer standing in the doorway with his bow. He had shot the Wolf and saved Red Riding Hood.

And what had happened to the real Grandmother? She was too thin for the Wolf to eat so he had gagged her and stuffed her in a shed in the garden.

Little Red Riding Hood never disobeyed her mother again.

queen
A **queen** is the ruler of a country, or the wife of a king. How many **queens** are there in this book?

quick
"Take this basket to your Grandmother," said Red Riding Hood's Mother. "And be very **quick** about it. Walk as fast as you can."

quiet
It was very **quiet** deep in the forest. Red Riding Hood could hear no sound as she gathered flowers for her Grandmother.

rabbit

A **rabbit** is a small furred animal with long ears and a tail like a white powder-puff.

race

When you run in a **race** you try to go faster than all the other children. You **race** them.

radio

A **radio** broadcasts programmes that you can listen to.

radish

A **radish** is a red and white salad vegetable.

rain

Rain is wet. It falls from the clouds in the sky to give us water.

rainbow

A **rainbow** is an arch of colours in the sky. You can see one when it is raining and sunny at the same time.

raincoat

It's a good idea to wear a **raincoat** on rainy days to keep you dry.

rattle

If you shake a chain the sound it makes is a **rattle**. Babies like the noise of **rattles**.

read

Can you **read** yet? You can if you are **reading** this book.

ready

"I am not **ready** to go to Grandmother's house just yet," said Red Riding Hood to herself. "I must finish picking this bunch of flowers first."

really

"Is this **really** my Grandmother?" thought Red Riding Hood. "It does not look quite like her."

red

Red is the colour of little **Red** Riding Hood's coat and hood.

remember

"**Remember** what I tell you, Red Riding Hood," said her Mother. "Make sure you go straight to your Grandmother's house. Do not forget."

rest

"Come and lie beside me and **rest** after your long walk," said the Wicked Wolf to Red Riding Hood. "You can tell me the **rest** of your news later."

rice

Rice is a grain that can be eaten instead of potato, or sweet in a rice pudding.

ride

"Would you like to **ride** on my back, little girl?" asked the Wolf. "You can sit on me and I will carry you to your Grandmother's house."

right

"You were quite **right**, Mother," said Red Riding Hood afterwards. "I should have kept to the path, as you said."

ring

A **ring** is a circle. You can wear **rings** on your fingers. You can join hands with all your friends and dance in a **ring**.

river

A **river** is a large stream of water. Little
Red Riding Hood was not far from the
river when she met the Wolf.

road

A **road** joins one place to another.
People and cars use **roads** to go to other
places.

robot

A **robot** is a machine that can do many
things a person can do.

rock

A **rock** is a very large stone.

rod

A **rod** is a straight stick made from
wood or metal. See how many **rods** you can find at your house.

roll

If little Red Riding Hood had dropped her basket the cakes would have **rolled** out everywhere. Round things like wheels **roll** along the ground. It's the way they move.

roof

A **roof** is a lid. The **roof** of Grandmother's cottage was made of slate. What is the **roof** of your house made of?

room

The inside of Grandmother's cottage was one big **room**. She (or rather the Wolf) was sitting up in bed when Red Riding Hood went in. How many **rooms** has your house?

round

A ball is **round**. A coin is **round**. What else is **round**?

row

It is fun to **row** a boat with oars. When you **row** the oars dip in and out of the water and help to push the boat along.

rub

To **rub** is to slide things together. **Rub** your hand on a brick wall. What do you feel?

rubber

Tyres are made of **rubber**. You can use a **rubber** to rub out pencil marks that are in the wrong place.

rubbish

Rubbish is waste. You don't want it any more so you throw it away. Sometimes other people can use your **rubbish**.

rug

There was a big thick **rug** on Grandmother's bed to keep her warm. There was a pretty round **rug** on the floor, too.

ruler

A **ruler** is a straight piece of wood or plastic for measuring and drawing straight lines.

run

The Wolf must have **run** very fast to reach Grandmother's cottage before little Red Riding Hood did. Do you like **running**?

The Sleeping Beauty

Ss

Long ago a King and Queen waited for many years before a daughter was born to them. They were so delighted that they invited everyone to the christening. Everyone, that is, except the thirteenth fairy who was known to be rather bad-tempered.

The christening-day arrived. All the guests, including the twelve fairies, lined up to give gifts to the baby Princess. All at once the door burst open. In came the thirteenth fairy. She was so cross at having been left out that she cast a spell on the baby.

"When the Princess is fifteen years old she will prick her finger on a spindle and die," she shouted.

Now the twelfth fairy had not yet given her present. She couldn't undo the spell but promised that the Princess would fall asleep for a hundred years, instead of dying.

At once all the spindles in the castle were destroyed. Then came the Princess's fifteenth birthday party. Everyone played hide-and-seek. The Princess found a little room at the top of an old tower where an old woman sat spinning. The Princess, who had never seen a spindle, was fascinated and asked if she could use it.

Of course, the next minute she had pricked her finger and fallen down asleep. Everybody else in the castle (except the wicked old woman) fell asleep too, just where they were.

Years went by and the thorned briers grew thick around the castle. One day a handsome Prince came riding by. He had heard the legend of the sleeping Princess Brier Rose and he wanted to go and see her for himself in spite of the thorns.

To his astonishment, the wild roses curled back and let him pass through to the castle. Inside, everybody was asleep. The Prince finally came to where the Pricess was lying. She looked so beautiful that he couldn't resist giving her a kiss.

At that moment Sleeping Beauty awoke and rubbed her eyes and asked what time it was. It was exactly one hundred years since she had pricked her finger.

Everyone in the castle awoke, and instead of a fifteenth birthday party, the feast became a wedding breakfast for the beautiful Princess Brier Rose and her handsome Prince.

sail

A **sail** on a **sailing** boat is a large piece of cloth that fills with wind. It makes the boat move and **sail** on the water.

sale

"Grand **sale** to-day!" That means that lots of things are going to be **sold**.

salt

Salt is white. You put it on food to bring out the flavour. **Salt** gives sea water its taste.

same

The Sleeping Princess and all the people at the Palace stayed the **same**, without change, for one hundred years. When the Princess pricked her finger they all fell asleep and didn't change until the Prince broke the spell.

sand

Beaches are full of **sand**. So are riverbeds and deserts. **Sand** is finely ground rock.

sandwich

Here's a little boy just about to eat a cheese **sandwich** at the Princess's party. It is two slices of bread with cheese in between.

Santa Claus

Santa Claus is another name for Saint Nicholas who brings presents at Christmas time to children.

Saturday

Saturday is the last day of the week. It comes after Friday.

sausage

A **sausage** is meat inside a skin. Look!
One of the dogs has fallen asleep
eating a **sausage**.

say

The twelfth fairy said, "I cannot undo
the spell, but I can soften it by **saying**
that the Princess will not die. She will
fall asleep for a hundred years." When
they heard her speak, the King and
Queen were not sure whether to be
glad or not.

scarf

A **scarf** is a long piece of cloth worn
around the neck.

scare

"Do not let the thirteenth fairy's spell
scare you," said the twelfth fairy. "She
wants to frighten you, but I can soften
the spell."

school

School is a place for learning new things and making new friends.

scratch

"You cannot enter the Palace," said the old man to the Prince. "The briers will **scratch** you and tear your skin."

screw

A **screw** is like a nail but instead of hitting it with a hammer you turn it round and round with a **screwdriver** until it is tight.

scribble

To **scribble** is to make patterns for fun with a pencil.

sea

The **sea** is the salty water all around the coast. It is deep and many fish live in it.

seat

Princess Brier Rose entered the cold stone room and saw an old woman sitting on a wooden **seat**.

second

The Princess took the spindle and tried to spin. The next **second** she had pricked herself and fallen down. (There are sixty **seconds** in a minute.) Luckily it was the **second** spell, spell number two, that was working and she fell asleep instead of dying.

secret
"There is a **secret** in that palace," said the Prince. "I must find it out so that everyone will know what has happened."

see
"I will go and **see** Brier Rose with my own eyes. I will not be happy until I have **seen** her."

seed
A **seed** grows in the middle of a fruit or flower. When it is planted a new plant grows. See how many **seeds** you can find in apples and oranges and other fruit in your house.

send
When you write a letter you can **send** it by post to its destination. Make sure you write the address clearly so that it is **sent** to the right place!

September
September is the ninth month of the year. It comes before October.

set
Hasn't the jelly on the table **set** well? It isn't runny at all. The maid has put out the best **set** of spoons to eat it with.

seven
Seven is 7.

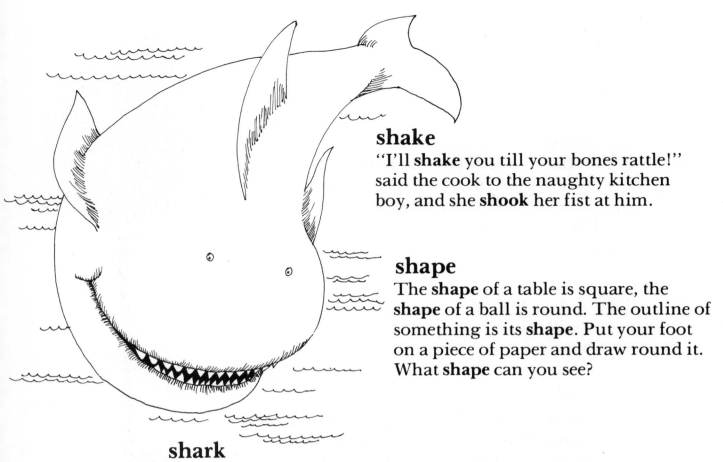

shake

"I'll **shake** you till your bones rattle!" said the cook to the naughty kitchen boy, and she **shook** her fist at him.

shape

The **shape** of a table is square, the **shape** of a ball is round. The outline of something is its **shape**. Put your foot on a piece of paper and draw round it. What **shape** can you see?

shark

A **shark** is a large fish with sharp teeth. It lives in the sea.

sharp

The **sharp** teeth of a shark are pointed and can cut into things easily, like a knife.

sheep

A **sheep** is a farm animal. Most **sheep** are white but some are black. **Sheep** wool is used to make warm clothes, blankets and carpets. Can you see anything made from the wool of **sheep**?

shell

A **shell** is a hard covering. Do you ever collect sea-**shells** on the beach? A soft sea-animal used to live inside the **shell**.

shift
To **shift** is to move.

ship
A **ship** carries people and cargo across the sea.

shirt
The Prince's **shirt** was made of fine silk.

shoes
His **shoes** were of soft leather. **Shoes** protect feet.

shoot
You can **shoot** an arrow from a bow or water from a water-pistol or a bullet from a gun. A **shot** is a very fast movement of something from one place to another.

shop
A **shop** sells things. You go to the **shops** to do your **shopping**.

short
Short is not long or not tall. Are you **shorter** than the top of the door? Are you as **short** as the handle on the door?

show
The wicked thirteenth fairy cast a spell on the Princess to **show** how cross she was at not being invited to the christening. She wanted everyone to see her anger.

131

shut

The Princess climbed to the top of the winding stairs and found that the door at the top was **shut**. It was closed and the Princess had to push hard to open it.

shy

As the Prince rode along, **shy** little birds hid in the trees at the side of the path. They did not want him to see them. They were timid.

sick

If you had seen inside the palace after everyone had fallen asleep you would have thought all the people were **sick**. They had all been asleep so long that it looked as though they were ill.

side

When Princess Brier Rose awoke she saw the Prince at her **side**. He was beside her.

silly

Wasn't the Princess **silly** to prick herself on that spindle? It was a very foolish thing to do.

sing

"**Sing** a Song of Sixpence!" Do you know that song? Do you like **singing**?

sister

Your **sister** is a girl who has the same
mother and father as you have. Have you a **sister**?

sit

"**Sit** down here and try your hand at
spinning," said the wicked fairy. She
sat down beside the Princess. While
they were **sitting** together Princess
Brier Rose pricked her finger and
then . . . You finish the story.

six

Six is 6.

skate

If you wear roller **skates** on your feet
you can **skate** over the ground quickly.
Roller **skates** have very small wheels
for rolling over the ground. Ice **skates**
are for **skating** on ice.

skip

"Salt, mustard, vinegar, pepper." Do
you play that **skipping** game? When
you **skip** you jump over the rope and
shout one of the words each time.

sky

Look out of the window. The **sky** is
way up above the buildings and trees.
Is it blue, or grey, or white and cloudy today?

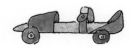

sleep

The Princess and all the palace went to **sleep** for one hundred years. Nothing would wake them until the hundred years were up.

slide

A **slide** is something to slip down. **Slides** are fun in the playground. You can **slide** on slippery mud, too.

slip

The wicked fairy knew that the Princess's finger would **slip** if she picked up the spindle. And sure enough, when the Princess touched the slippery spindle her finger **slid** straight on to the point.

slow

Slow is not fast. A tortoise moves **slowly**.

small

Small is little. A cat is **smaller** than a horse. It is not as big.

smash

Take care when you drink from a glass. If you drop it, it will **smash** into thousands of pieces.

smell
The Prince kissed the Sleeping Beauty. Soon the whole palace was awake and everyone's nose could **smell** beautiful food. The Cook was preparing the wedding dinner.

snail
A **snail** is a very small soft animal that lives in a shell. He carries his house around with him on his back.

snake
A **snake** is a long slim reptile with no legs. It slides along the ground.

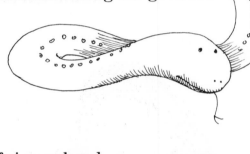

sock
A **sock** is worn on a foot and inside a shoe.

soft
A kitten's fur and a baby's skin are **soft**. **Soft** is not hard.

some
Some of the sleepers in the Palace were lying on the floor. Not all of them, but a few of them.

somebody
Somebody was asleep on the kitchen table.

something
Something could be seen behind the curtain.

sometimes

Sometimes people would try to enter the Palace and discover the secret of Brier Rose.

somewhere

Somewhere, far away, the Prince was riding towards the Palace.

soon

Soon the long sleep would be over. It would not be long now.

sore

When the Princess woke up her finger was still **sore** where she had pricked it. It hurt a little bit.

sorry

The Prince asked the old man the way to the Palace. "You will be **sorry** if you try to go in," warned the old man. "You will wish you hadn't tried."

136

sort

The maid had to **sort** out the knives and forks and arrange them on the table, ready for the feast.

soup

Chicken, beef, minestrone, spring onion. What flavour **soup** do you like best to keep out the cold on winter days?

space

Space has nothing in it that you can see. Is there much **space** in your house? Is there room to move?

spaceship

A **spaceship** is a machine that goes up into outer space. It circles round the earth. There is plenty of room to move in outer space.

speak

For a hundred years no one spoke a word in the Palace. They couldn't **speak** because they were all asleep. Just imagine not being able to say anything for a hundred years!

spell

In fairy tales a witch often casts a magic **spell** on someone. What **spell** did the thirteenth fairy cast on Princess Brier Rose? In real life you learn to **spell** words. **Spelling** is saying which letter comes next in a word.

spider

A **spider** is a tiny animal with eight legs. **Spiders** spin webs to catch insects to eat.

spill

The maid was lucky that she didn't **spill** the wine when she fell asleep. She could easily have dropped the bottle and the wine would have gone all over the floor.

spin

The Princess wanted to learn to **spin** wool, like the old woman. **Spinning** is turning something very quickly. If you twist fleece very quickly you **spin** it into woollen thread.

splash

Splash! The kitchen-boy dropped the
potato in the water. He'd been holding
it for a hundred years!

spoon

A **spoon** is for eating soup and jelly
and cornflakes with. It's for stirring tea
and porridge too. What else?

sport

A **sport** is a game. Football, softball
and cricket are **sports**. Which is your favourite **sport**?

spot

A **spot** is a small mark. The maid is
wearing a dress with **spots** on.

square

All four sides of a **square** are the same
length. How many **squares** can you
find around you?

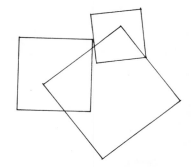

stair

A **stair** is a step. Princess Brier Rose
climbed up the **stairs** of the tower to hide from her friends.

stand

To **stand** is to be upright. The horses in the Palace stables fell asleep **standing** up. They didn't lie down. The Princess's birthday cake **stood** on the table for one hundred years.

start

When the Prince kissed the Sleeping Beauty she **started** to wake up. Everyone in the Palace began to wake up. The king woke with a **start** when the kitchen-boy knocked the saucepan on to the floor.

stay

Can you **stay** still for five minutes? Can you not move at all for that long?

steal

To **steal** is to take something that doesn't belong to you. You take it without the owner knowing.

step

The Princess took small **steps** as she danced at her wedding. She didn't move her feet very far each time.

stick

If you break a cup or a toy you can ask Daddy to **stick** it together with glue. In fairy stories there is often a witch who rides on a **broomstick**. Is there one in this story?

still

Still is not moving. Everything in the Palace was **still** for a hundred years.

stir

The Cook was just about to **stir** the soup when she fell asleep. She had put the spoon in to mix it around.

stomach

Your **stomach** is where your food goes to be digested. Cook has a very large **stomach**!

stone

The Palace was built of **stone**. Go out in the garden. How many small **stones** can you find on the ground?

stop

"**Stop**!" cried the old man to the Prince. "Do not go any nearer the Palace. It is dangerous. Stay here!" To **stop** is to become still.

story

What you read at the beginning of the letter S is the **story** of the Sleeping Beauty.

straight

Straight is not curvy. It is like the edge of this book.

straw

The horses had lots of **straw** in their stables to keep them warm. **Straw** is dried corn or barley or wheat stalks.

strawberry

A **strawberry** is a small red fruit.

street

A **street** is a road with houses on each side.

string

String is very useful for tying things up. Find some **string** and practise tying knots.

strong

Firm, healthy, tough, solid. **Strong** is all these things. Have you enough **strength** to lift what this **strong** man is lifting?

such

It was **such** a long way to the Palace that the Prince had to stop and give his horse a drink.

sugar

Sugar is sweet. It goes into cakes and drinks to sweeten them.

sum

What is the answer to this **sum:** 3 + 4?
And this one: 2 − 1?

sun

The **sun** gives us warmth and light. It is a long way from earth, in space.

Sunday

Sunday is the first day of the week.

suppose

To **suppose** is to think. What do you **suppose** the Princess said when she woke up?

sure

"Are you **sure** you want to go to the Palace?" said the old man to the Prince. "It's very dangerous. Do you really want to go?"

swan

A **swan** is a large white bird with a long graceful neck.

swim

Swans **swim** in lakes and rivers. This swan is **swimming** in a river near the Palace. Can you swim?

swing

Swing your arms, move them to and fro, in time to the music. Have fun at the Princess's wedding.

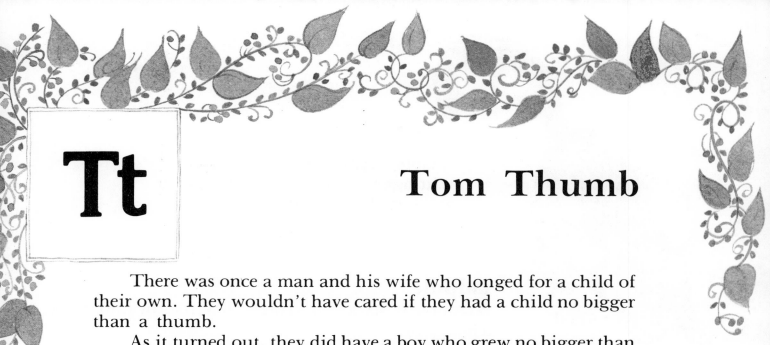

Tt

Tom Thumb

There was once a man and his wife who longed for a child of their own. They wouldn't have cared if they had a child no bigger than a thumb.

As it turned out, they did have a boy who grew no bigger than a thumb. They called him Tom Thumb. He was a fine brave little fellow. One day he showed his father how he could drive the horse and cart by clinging on to the horse's bridle and shouting into its ear. Two men saw this and offered the father a bag of gold in return for his son.

Tom told his father to accept, and rode off on the hat of one of the men. They were robbers who wanted Tom to creep through the iron bars of the parson's window to pass out all his valuables.

They arrived at the parson's house, and Tom talked so loudly that the maid awoke. She screamed. The robbers fled and Tom found a bundle of hay to sleep in.

Unluckily for him, the hay was for the cow to eat, which she did, and Tom went down with it. Down in the cow's stomach it was very dark and hot and stuffy, and it was filling up with hay very rapidly.

Tom cried out, "Don't give me any more hay!" The maid thought the cow was bewitched.

The parson came and shot the cow, whose stomach was put on a rubbish heap. Tom had just about found his way out when along came a Wolf to gulp him down along with the cow's stomach!

Tom told the Wolf that he could show him a house where there was plenty to eat, and he told him how to get to his own father's house. By the time they arrived there it was night-time so Tom told the Wolf to squeeze in through the bars on the pantry window.

The Wolf ate and ate until he was nearly bursting, and tried to squeeze out through the bars again. But he was too fat and got stuck.

In the morning Tom's father saw the Wolf and cut off his head with an axe. Then out jumped Tom Thumb, to the surprise and delight of his parents, who never sold him again.

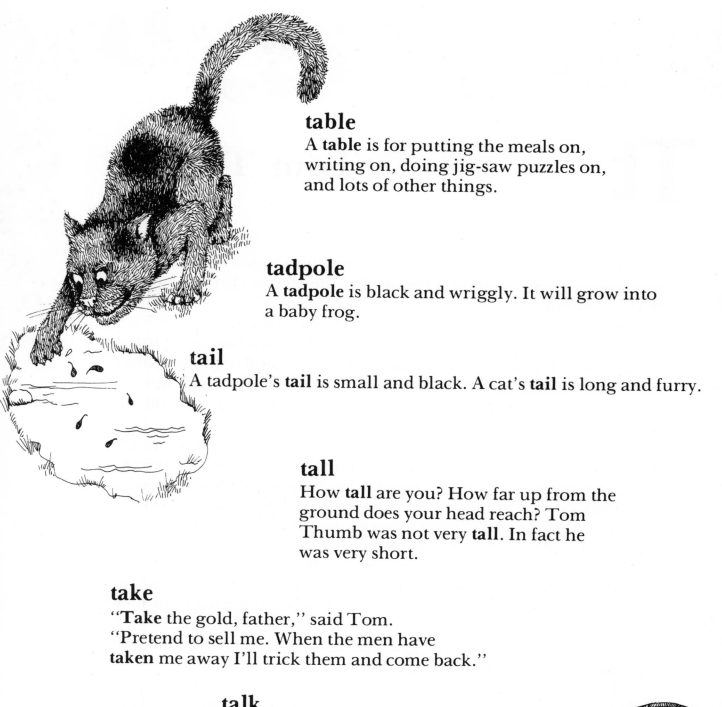

table

A **table** is for putting the meals on,
writing on, doing jig-saw puzzles on,
and lots of other things.

tadpole

A **tadpole** is black and wriggly. It will grow into
a baby frog.

tail

A tadpole's **tail** is small and black. A cat's **tail** is long and furry.

tall

How **tall** are you? How far up from the
ground does your head reach? Tom
Thumb was not very **tall**. In fact he
was very short.

take

"**Take** the gold, father," said Tom.
"Pretend to sell me. When the men have
taken me away I'll trick them and come back."

talk

"Hush! Don't **talk** so loudly," said the
robbers to Tom Thumb. "If you speak
like that someone will hear you."

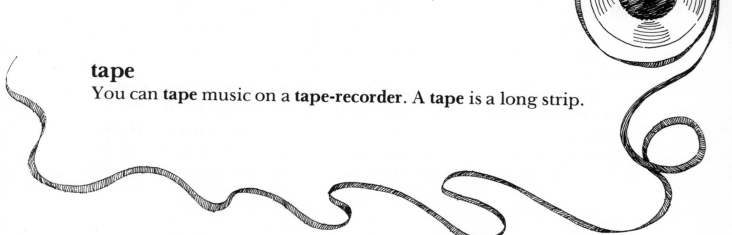

tape

You can **tape** music on a **tape-recorder**. A **tape** is a long strip.

tea

Tea is a drink made of dried leaves and
hot water. Do you like it with milk and sugar?

teach

This book will **teach** you some new words. You will learn them from it.

tear

To **tear** is to rip. After all his
adventures Tom's suit was **torn** and spoilt.

teeth

Teeth cut and chew. How lucky Tom
was not to get chewed up by the Wolf's
sharp **teeth**!

telephone

A **telephone** is for talking to someone who is far away.

television

You can watch programmes that are
being broadcast a long way away on
television.

tell

"I can **tell** you how to get a house with
all the food you want in it," said Tom
to the Wolf. When Tom had **told** him
how to get there, the Wolf set off.

ten

Ten is 10.

147

tennis

Tennis is a game. You hit a ball with a racquet over a net.

test

To **test** is to try out. **Test** yourself on the story of Tom Thumb — do you know it all?

than

Tom Thumb is much smaller **than** the tennis ball on this page, isn't he?

thank

"**Thank** you for getting me out of the wolf, Father," said Tom. "I am very **thankful** to be back home again."

there

"**There** is something strange going on over **there**," said one of the men. "**There** is a horse and cart with no one driving it, but I can hear a voice speaking!"

these

These are mine and **those** are yours.

thing

"What a strange **thing**," said the two men. "A tiny man as small as a thumb. We should be able to do **something** with him that will make us lots of money." What was it that the two men wanted to do with Tom Thumb?

think

"Don't worry Father," said Tom. "I **think** I know how to trick these men. I have **thought** of a good idea."

this

This is here and **that** is there.

though

Even **though** Tom had been inside a cow and inside a wolf he was still as cheerful as ever.

three

Three is 3.

through

The wolf had eaten so many cakes that he could not squeeze **through** the pantry window. Only his head would go **through** it. (The rest of him was stuck.)

throw

Do you like playing catch? You **throw** the ball to someone who has to catch it.

thumb

Your **thumb** is the short finger on your hand. It is apart from the other four fingers. Tom **Thumb** grew no bigger than his mother's **thumb**!

Thursday
Thursday is the fifth day of the week.

tidy
Tom Thumb looks very **tidy** and neat in his new suit, doesn't he?

tie
Can you **tie** up your shoe-laces? To **tie** is to knot together.

tiger
A **tiger** is a very large cat. It is striped and is very fierce.

tight
"Hold on **tight**," called Tom's mother as he rode away on the horse. Tom hung on to the horse's bridle so that he would not fall off.

time
"What a long **time** you have been away, Tom," said his father. "Are you all right?" "Don't worry, father," said Tom. "I am glad to be home. What **time** is it? I am so hungry it must be **dinnertime**."

tiny
Tiny is very small, like Tom Thumb.

tip

After his adventures, Tom was untidy from the top of his hat to the **tip** of his toes.

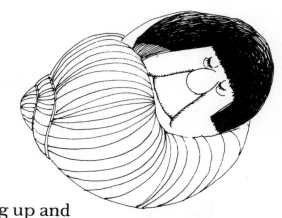

tired

Tom was so **tired** after walking up and down the ploughed furrows that he was glad to find a snail shell. He curled up in it and went straight to sleep.

toast

Toast is bread cooked under the grill or in a **toaster**. Honey is nice on **toast**.

today

Today is the day that started this morning.

toe

How many **toes** are there on your feet? There should be ten.

together

The two robbers ran away **together** when the maid shouted, "Help! Thieves!" They both ran away at the same time.

tomato
A **tomato** is a red, juicy vegetable that tastes good in a salad.

tomorrow
Tomorrow is the day after today.

tonight
Tonight is the evening of today. "**Tonight**, when the sun has gone down, I can show you where to get lots of food," said Tom to the greedy Wolf.

tooth
A **tooth** is for biting. The Wolf's **teeth** are much bigger than yours, aren't they?

top
Tom Thumb slid from the **top** of the robber's hat to the brim. He could sit there safely without falling off.

touch
Touch the picture of the tomato. Put your finger on it and feel it. Do you think the Wolf got through the window without **touching** the sides?

two
Two is 2.

UuVv

The Ugly Duckling

A large mother duck was rather tired of sitting on her eggs day after day and waiting for them to hatch. She was very pleased when they finally started to hatch, all except one which was much bigger than the others. It took much longer, and when a duckling finally emerged it was big and grey and ugly. Not at all like all her other fluffy ducklings.

As the days went by it seemed that the farmyard animals did not like the Ugly Duckling because he was different from the others. He was pecked and scolded and set upon all day long and he became very unhappy.

The Ugly Duckling could bear it no longer and left his unkind family. As he walked sadly along by the river he heard strange cries above him. He looked up and saw six of the most beautiful large white birds that he had ever seen. They were flying gracefully, their great white wings flapping slowly, and their long elegant necks stretched out in front of them. The Ugly Duckling thought he had never seen such a sight and he watched them as long as he could. Then he crept into the reeds, put his head under his wings and slept, dreaming of the beautiful white birds.

Winter came and the weather grew very cold. One day it was so cold that the river froze over, and the poor little Ugly Duckling froze too. Luckily for him a passing farmer saw him and carried him home to his farmhouse. There, in the warmth, he revived, but the children rushed at him, wanting to play. He was frightened. He upset the milk and the flour, and was shouted at by the farmer's wife. He flew away from the farmhouse in terror and took refuge in the bushes.

When he had recovered his strength he rose up and spread his wings and flew. As he flew the weather grew warmer and the sun began to shine. Below him he saw three white swans on a lake. He knew he must join them even though they might be unfriendly.

But they welcomed him! He soon understood why when he looked down and saw his reflection in the water. The Ugly Duckling had turned into a beautiful swan.

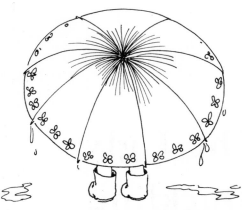

umbrella
An **umbrella** keeps the rain off you.

uncle
Your **uncle** is the brother of your father or mother.

under
The Ugly Duckling crept **under** the rushes to hide from the ducks and geese who laughed at him. He hid his head **underneath** his wings.

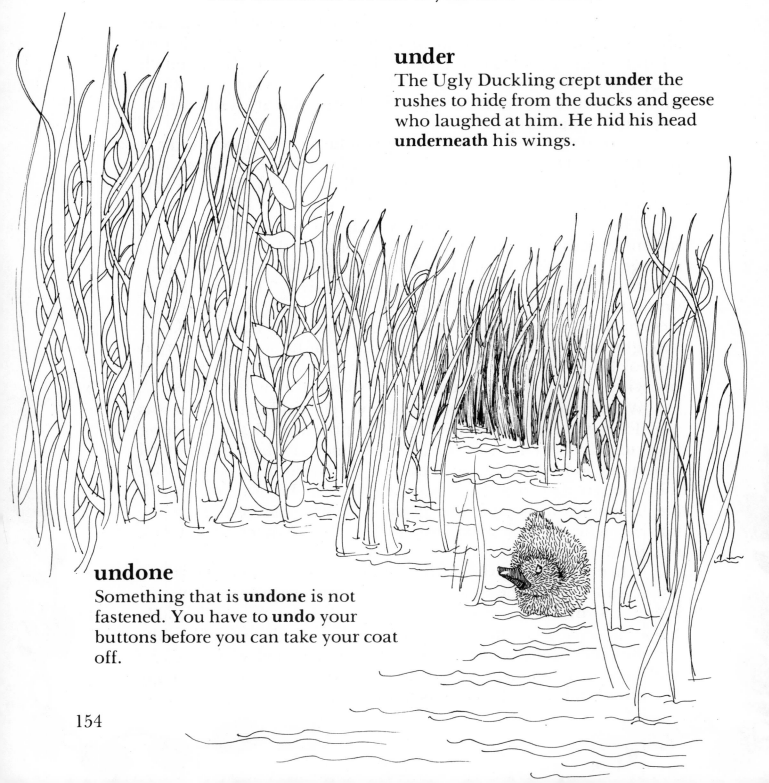

undone
Something that is **undone** is not fastened. You have to **undo** your buttons before you can take your coat off.

until

The Ugly Duckling didn't know he was a beautiful swan **until** he saw his reflection in the water. Then he could see how he had changed.

up

The Ugly Duckling looked **up** into the sky at the swans flying past.

upstairs

The farmer went **upstairs** to tell his children about the duckling he had found. The children rushed down to see it.

use

The Ugly Duckling would **use** the rushes to hide in. He had got **used** to all the other ducks and hens pecking at him and being rude.

vanish

Sometimes the Ugly Duckling wished he could just **vanish** completely. He wanted to disappear suddenly and be invisible.

vegetables

Carrots, cabbages, onions, potatoes, lettuces. All these things are **vegetables**. Think of some more.

veranda

A **veranda** is the long, narrow, open part of a house with a roof held up by pillars. It stops the sun from making the house too hot.

very

"This duckling is **very** ugly," said the hen. "He is too ugly to stay in this farmyard."

violin

A **violin** is a musical instrument. A person who plays a **violin** is a **violinist**.

voice

You speak and sing and shout with your **voice**. The Ugly Duckling cried out in a coarse loud **voice** when he saw the swans flying overhead.

Ww

The White Swans

Once upon a time there lived a King who had eleven sons and one daughter, called Elise. They were all very happy until the King married a Queen who was a very cruel and wicked witch. She told the King lies about his sons so that he no longer loved them; and then she turned them into swans. To get rid of Elise she smeared her face with walnut stain to make her ugly. The King was shocked and could not speak to Elise.

The sad princess went off to look for her brothers. The Queen's spell was such that at night they were men and in the daytime they became swans. An old woman helped Elise find them and they took her to the country where they lived. Elise dreamt that if she wove a nettle shirt for each brother, and did not speak a word until they were done, the spell would be broken.

Elise immediately began the work, but she had only made three shirts when a King passed by and fell in love with her. He carried her to his palace and she spoke no word.

Every night she went to a cellar to continue her work, but the Archbishop followed her. He looked in the cellar and told the King about the nettle yarn and shirt he had seen.

The King thought Elise must be a witch and ordered her to be burnt. Meanwhile, she was locked in the cellar where she finished making the nettle shirts. When the guard came to put her in a cart to take her to her death she picked up all the shirts and carried them with her.

As the cart went through the palace gates Elise saw her brothers flying overhead. She waved to them and they flew down beside her. She flung the shirts over the swans and they became princes again.

The King was overjoyed to hear that his wife was not a witch, and Elise was very happy to have her brothers back again.

wait

The white swans had to **wait** until the
sun set before they were changed back
to princes.

wake

To **wake** is to stop sleeping. When
Elise **woke** up from her dream she
knew that she had to weave eleven
shirts for her brothers.

walk

Every night Elise would **walk** quietly
to the cellar to finish weaving the
shirts for her brothers. But one night
the Archbishop saw her **walking** back
to her room. To **walk** is to move by
using feet, one after the other.

wall

The King's palace was surrounded by a
very high **wall** made of stones so that
no one could see into the palace garden.

wallaby

A **wallaby** is a furry Australian animal.
It is like a kangaroo but smaller.

want

"I **want** you to leave the palace," the
wicked Queen said to the eleven
Princes. "I will change you into white
swans so that my wish will come true."
To be **in want** is to need something.

warm

It was **warm** in the cave where the eleven swans lived. It was not cold.

wash

Elise had to **wash** her face to clean off
the brown walnut stain. When she had
washed herself she looked beautiful
again.

watch

Elise sat down by the stream to **watch**
for the white swans. Soon she saw
them flying through the air.

water

Without **water** nothing can live. Seas
and rivers and clouds and
underground wells are full of **water**.
Sea **water** tastes salty. Drinking **water**
has little taste and no colour.

wave

The eleven white swans saw Elise **wave**
to them from the cart. They saw her
handkerchief fluttering in the breeze.
Waves crash on to the beach. Surf-
riders like them.

way

"This is the **way** to the place where I
saw the swans," said the old woman to
Elise. "You follow this path to get
there."

wear

Elise knew that if the swans could **wear**
her nettle shirts they would change
back into princes. They had to put the
shirts on.

web

In the morning you may see a spider's
web hanging from the bushes. The
spider weaves his **web** to catch flies in.
Then he eats the flies.

Wednesday

Wednesday is the fourth day of the week. What day is it today?

week

How many days in a **week**? There are seven. Can you name them?

well

Elise wove the nettle shirts very **well**. She was good at weaving.
A **well** is a place where water can be drawn up from underground.

west

Every evening the sun sets in the **west**. Look out for the setting sun
tonight to see where **west** is.

wet

Elise cried when she was turned out of
the palace. The tears made her face **wet**.

what

"**What** is the matter?" asked the old
woman. She could see Elise was
unhappy but she didn't know **what** the
reason was.

wheel

A **wheel** is round and it rolls along the
ground. Cars, bicycles, lorries, trains,
aeroplanes. All these things need
wheels to make them move properly.

when

"**When** the sun rises we are swans,"
said the eldest brother. "Later, **when** it
sets, we are princes again. At what time
will we be free of this spell?"

where

The princes decided to take Elise back to the land **where** they lived.

which

"**Which** one of us can carry her on his
back?" they said. "I can do it," said the
fourth brother.

while

The princes decided to carry Elise away
in the morning. **While** it was daytime
they were swans and they could fly a
long way. **While** means as long as, or
at the same time.

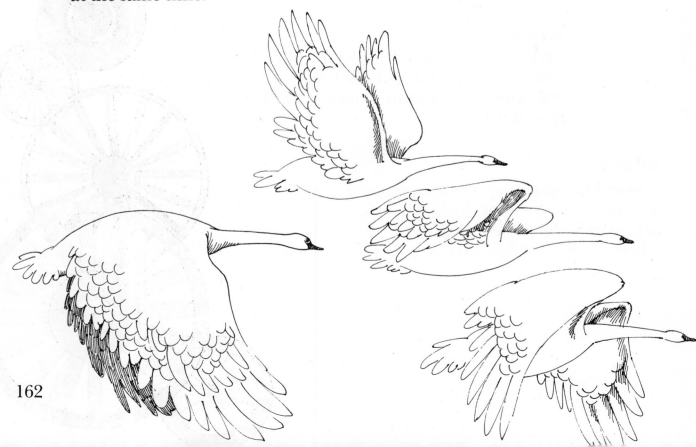

whistle

Can you **whistle**? That's the noise you can make through your teeth and lips, with your mouth in a small o. Stationmasters have a special **whistle**.

white

White is the colour of this page, where it has no writing or pictures on it.

who

"I have found out **who** Elise really is," said the Archbishop to the King. "She is a witch."

whole

When Elise threw the shirts on to the eleven swans they changed into princes again. Then she was able to tell the King the **whole** story. She could tell him everything that had happened since she had been thrown out by her wicked stepmother.

why

"**Why** are there such cruel people in the world?" asked the King. "I wonder what the reason is."

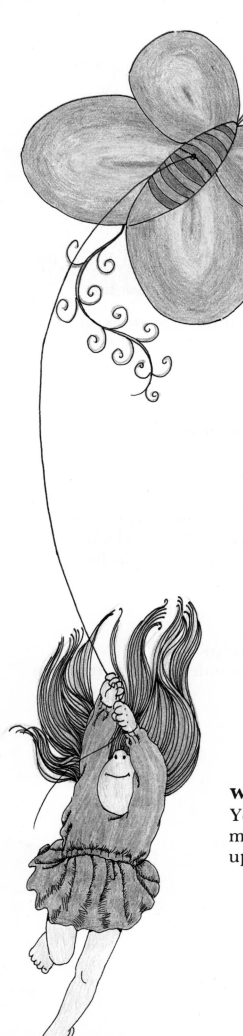

will

"It doesn't matter now," replied Elise. "We **will** be able to live in peace and happiness for ever."

win

Do you have races with your friends? Do you like to **win**? The **winner** is always the person who comes first.

wind

Sometimes the **wind** blows very strongly. It is moving air. It is fun to fly a kite on a **windy** day.

window

The cellar where Elise sat and wove the nettle shirts had only one small **window**. It was just a small open space in the wall where the light could come through. What can you see through your **window**?

wipe

You **wipe** wet things with a cloth to make them dry. Do you help to **wipe** up after dinner?

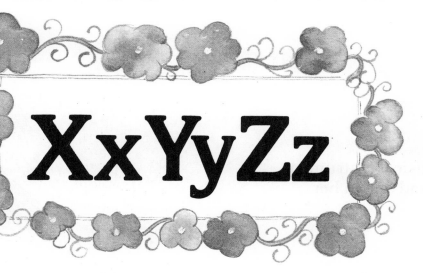

XxYyZz

Rapunzel

There was once a man whose wife was about to have a child for whom they had both longed for many years. One day the wife had a craving for some green rampion which she saw growing in the garden of a witch. She told her husband he *must* climb over the wall and get her some.

The husband did as he was told with great reluctance — and sure enough the witch caught him. She would let him go only on the condition that when the baby was born it would be given to her. And so it was.

When the child, named Rapunzel, was twelve years old the witch took her and locked her in the top of a tower. Its only entrance was through a small high window. When the witch wanted to go in she would shout, "Rapunzel, let down your hair." Then she climbed up the thick golden plaits to the window.

Rapunzel had spent several years in the tower, when one day a Prince rode by. He heard her singing and tried to find a way into the tower, but could not. Then the witch appeared, and as the Prince lay hidden in the bushes, he saw her climb up Rapunzel's hair to enter the tower.

He waited until the witch had gone out again, and then called, "Rapunzel, let down your hair." In no time he was in the tower with Rapunzel. He promised to bring her some silk which she could weave into a ladder and so escape.

But the witch found out about the Prince and chopped off Rapunzel's hair, and spirited the girl into a far-off wilderness. The poor Prince was so grief-stricken that he carelessly had an accident in which he was blinded.

He, too, was left to wander around by himself in loneliness.

Years passed and the Prince eventually came to the wilderness where Rapunzel was. He recognised her sweet singing and called to her. She ran to him and her tears of joy fell on his eyes. Instantly he was able to see again, and he took Rapunzel to his own kingdom and married her.

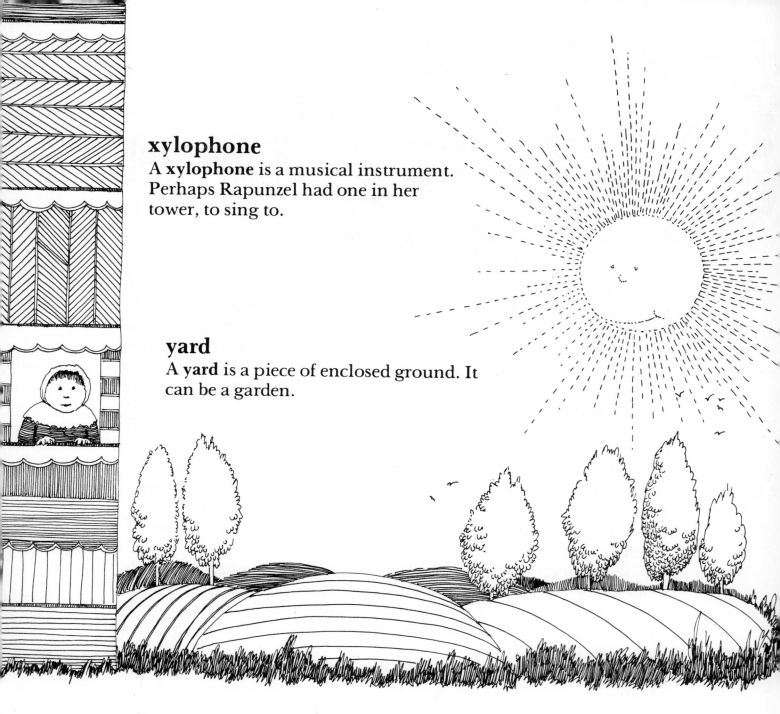

xylophone
A **xylophone** is a musical instrument. Perhaps Rapunzel had one in her tower, to sing to.

yard
A **yard** is a piece of enclosed ground. It can be a garden.

year
A **year** is twelve months or fifty-two weeks. In one **year** we have spring, summer, autumn and winter.

yellow
Yellow is the colour of sunflowers and wattle.

yes
When the Prince asked Rapunzel if she would marry him she said, "**Yes**, I will, I would like to."

yesterday
Yesterday is the day before today. If today is Wednesday, **yesterday** was Tuesday, and the day before that was . . .

yet
The Prince visits Rapunzel in her tower every evening. The old witch hasn't caught him **yet** — that was still to happen.

zebra

A **zebra** is an animal like a horse but
with black and white stripes. It lives in Africa.

zero

Zero is nothing. **Zero** is 0. **Zero** degrees
is very cold!

zip

You can fasten a dress or trousers with
a **zip**. Do it quickly — "**Zip!**" That's
the sharp, light sound Rapunzel made
when the witch whisked her through
the air to the far-off wilderness.

zoo

Lots of different animals live at the
zoo. They come from all over the world.

A B C

H I J K L

P Q R S T

Z-Z-Z-Z-Z-Z-Z